Dutch FlowerPot QUILTS

Townrow, Anja

 American Quilter's Society
P. O. Box 3290 • Paducah, KY 42002-3290
www.AQSquilt.com

Located in Paducah, Kentucky, the American Quilter's Society (AQS) is dedicated to promoting the accomplishments of today's quilters. Through its publications and events, AQS strives to honor today's quiltmakers and their work and to inspire future creativity and innovation in quiltmaking.

EDITOR: MARJORIE L. RUSSELL
GRAPHIC DESIGN: LYNDA SMITH
COVER DESIGN: MICHAEL BUCKINGHAM
PHOTOGRAPHY: CHARLES R. LYNCH

Library of Congress Cataloging-in-Publication Data
Townrow, Anja.
        Dutch flower pot quilts / by Anja Townrow.
                        p.   cm.
        ISBN 1-57432-766-6
        1. Patchwork--Patterns. 2. Patchwork quilts. 3. Flower pots in art.
I. Title.
TT835 .T67 2001   2000
746.46'041--dc21   200100984

Additional copies of this book may be ordered from the American Quilter's Society, PO Box 3290, Paducah, KY 42002-3290, or online at www.AQSquilt.com.

Dedication

For my daughters –

Ansie,

Harriet,

and Alice

Contents

Introduction

The famous bulb fields in Holland's Keukenhof region may be the subconscious source of inspiration for the designs in this book. Although I don't think I've ever visited The Keukenhof, I do remember seeing the vast fields of flowers as we traveled past them on family outings.

My favorite flowers were closer to home and more tangible. They were growing in the flower pots on my mother's windowsills. The typical Dutch custom of arranging a profusion of plants in front of the window, with a hand-crocheted net curtain proudly displayed above, is now my only link to the country where I was born and grew up.

As soon as I had my own home in England, I set about collecting the decorative over-pots that are essential to show off houseplants to their best advantage. Any passer-by cannot be in doubt about my nationality!

During my early years in England I became interested in growing geraniums, with their gorgeous colors and many varied leaves. When we moved to a house with a large, beautiful garden, I tended it lovingly and learned a lot about growing plants and how to design a flower border.

However, it was not long before quilting got me in its powerful grip, and these days the only flowers I tend are of the quilted variety! That change represents a very gradual process. I have been making patchwork for a long time, but only in the last four years has the neglect of my house and garden become noticeable. And it is now so bad that even I cannot ignore the sad signs any longer.

This spring, when half a dozen of my plants had to be thrown into the trash, I suddenly realized I had stopped looking after them, not even noticing that they were suffering, until it was too late. Instead, I'd made three quilts featuring flower pot patterns, with yet another nearly completed, and two more on the drawing board. Clearly, my interest in flowers was still there, but it had shifted. Poor bedraggled specimens of living plants in pots can now be seen struggling on my windowsills, while abundant, vibrant, and glowing pots of fabric flowers are found on every wall.

Even as a patchwork beginner, I was interested in curved piecing, and I've made many quilts featuring patterns such as Fans, Drunkard's Path, New York Beauty, Pickle Dish, etc. Then, as I discovered the wonders of foundation piecing, I started to draw designs that combined both techniques. Flower pot pictures, with their plump, curvy pots containing spiky plants with sharp points, were ideal for my purpose. I've selected some of my flower pot patterns for the collection in this book, and I hope you will get lasting enjoyment from them.

The patterns in this book will suit quilters of all skill levels. From the simple TULIP POT to the more complicated DAISY POT, there's bound to be a design to suit you. Along with the seven blocks featured in POT LUCK SAMPLER, you will find two "bonus" patterns, that were simply too nice to leave out.

Foundation piecing is the main technique used, with some blocks being entirely foundation pieced, while others involve some curved piecing to assemble the block parts. Some blocks share the same shape and size, and are

interchangeable within the quilt settings shown. Watch for mix-and-match suggestions in the relevant project sections.

Most of the quilts shown are small wall-hangings, but the blocks can easily be used for larger projects like bed quilts. Adjust the size of blocks to suit your purposes by reducing or enlarging patterns on a photocopier.

Make quick gifts by using any of the blocks to sew a cushion, bag or a small picture. Remember, your houseplants may have wilted from neglect, but your quilts will endure!

POT ROSE
72" x 72"

"The Mother of all Pot Plants" is a phrase coined by my friend Ruth Goodman for this quilt. This was the first Flower Pot quilt I designed as a vehicle to combine the techniques of curved piecing with foundation piecing. The batik fabric used in the background was a bit of a luxury item at the time, and I used home-dyed fabrics as well as quilters' cottons for the rest of the quilt. The quilting was done with invisible thread in parallel lines; I was not confident enough at that stage to try anything more adventurous!

REACHING FOR THE SUN

22" x 28"

When POT ROSE received international recognition, I was asked by the editor of THE QUILTER, the magazine of the Quilters' Guild of the British Isles, to design a project for her readers incorporating the techniques used in POT ROSE. The result was REACHING FOR THE SUN, a design that represents a "cutting" from POT ROSE. This quilt has become the subject of a very popular workshop, with many students producing their own unique versions.

NOSTALGIA

60" x 70"

NOSTALGIA was made in 1998 for a national quilt show in the United Kingdom. Theme of the show was "House and Home." NOSTALGIA depicts a very "Dutch" home, where English is spoken. A variety of handicrafts are displayed in this quilt: a cross-stitch picture, hand-crocheted curtain, broderie perse vases, and colorwash patchwork. I never once got bored while making this project!

Selecting Fabrics

"Where do you get your fabrics?" or "How do you pick your colors?" are the questions I hear most often from fellow quilters. I could offer a lengthy explanation, but the answer can really be given in one word: instinct. No matter how long I study books that contain in-depth analysis of the use of color, showing the color wheel and various charts, I never seem to be able to put any of my new knowledge into practice. Extensive reading on the subject has given me a grasp of some basic rules, but when it comes to choosing colors for my quilts, instinct takes over. As soon as I think about rules and theory, I get into trouble and become positively paralyzed, suddenly unable to put any two fabrics together.

So if your total theoretical knowledge of color amounts to the fact that blue and yellow make green, don't despair and don't feel you are "hopeless with color." Choosing fabrics and colors is just a matter of personal taste. Be confident of your color choices. If you like it, then use it.

Here are some useful fabric selection tips:

- Choose a printed fabric that you really like and pick out the colors in the print for the rest of the fabrics in the quilt. To add interest, introduce a "surprise" color into the scheme.
- Resist the tendency to over match fabrics. Adding a clashing, totally different fabric to a "matching" selection can add vibrancy to your Flower Pot blocks. Keep that in mind when selecting colors, and add the unexpected.
- Try anything that catches your eye. As soon as you spot a fabric on the shelf that looks promising, put it with your other selections. Don't dismiss a strange, strongly-patterned fabric; instead, ask yourself how you can make it work

for you. Perhaps you could cut a motif from it to appliqué onto a pot or into the center of a quilt to provide an interesting focal point for the piece.

- Make small quilts at first, so it is not a disaster if you don't like them. They will still be a much appreciated present or donation to charity. Put it down to experience and move on to the next quilt with a better idea of how you want to use colors in your new project.
- You could also choose your background fabric first. Many of the quilts in this book use strong, bright fabrics as backgrounds. That means that the rest of the colors have to be fairly powerful to stand out against the background.
- Do your own thing and don't listen to prevailing "wisdom." For example, a few years ago, it became accepted as common knowledge among quilters that yellow is a difficult color to use. Is that based on fact, or rumor? Find out for yourself! Perhaps you'll find that yellow is not so difficult after all.
- Consider stripes and border fabrics! These designs always work very hard to pay for their keep. In fact, many of the quilts pictured in this book rely heavily on striped fabric for their impact. When a striped design stands on its own in a pot or border, it also often allows the quilter to do less piecing. Stripes and border fabrics have worked so well for me that when I see a nice striped or border fabric, I purchase at least two yards of it to add to my collection.
- When choosing fabrics for Flower Pot quilts, avoid using too much green in the pots, as you will then be struggling to find something suitable for the leaves. Pick an accent color for use in the pot that can be brought back into the flowerhead, thus creating a balance in the design.

DECO POTS
52" x 51"

This was meant to be a black and white quilt, but more colors crept in while it was being made. The clear yellow, orange, blue, and green work well with the original choice of gray, black, and white.

Selecting Fabrics

SECOND CUTTING
24" x 28"

Both Flower Pots shown here are good examples of the way stripes do some of the work for you. In the borders as well as in the pots and fan-shaped parts, the stripes have been placed with care and forethought.

POT PLANT
24" x 28"

A riot of colors and fabrics make this quilt perhaps too lively for some tastes. It is definitely not boring!

CHINA POTS
62" x 62"

The orange batik combines with blue, green, and purple to make an unusual design. The original idea came from traditional American four-block quilts. Four large blocks that combine foundation piecing with curved piecing form the center of this prize winner.

PATIO POTS
48" x 52"

This quilt was designed as a project for the summer issue of a patchwork magazine. With sunny, bright colors and a center hole for an umbrella pole, this tablecloth is perfect for outdoors. You may even need sunglasses to look at this quilt! Once the striped fabric was chosen, selecting the rest of the colors presented no problem – they almost jumped off the shelves to join the pile!

Equipment

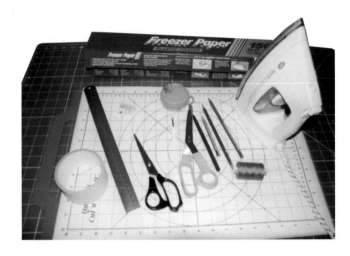

To make the projects in this book, only very basic equipment is required.

Paper scissors
Sharp dressmaking scissors
Seam ripper
Freezer paper – For tracing foundation piecing patterns, plastic-coated white freezer paper works well because the patches stick to the shiny side when ironed. Some of the blocks have large floppy patches which benefit from being secured to the paper during the foundation piecing so they cannot roll back and creep into the next line of stitching. Making the rest of the templates required for blocks can be done quickly and accurately by tracing the pattern onto freezer paper.
Pen – To trace lines on freezer paper that show through to the shiny side of the paper as well, a fine line marker pen works well. A ball-point pen could smudge onto your fingers and then onto your fabric, not to mention your machine, ironing pad, and clothes.

Ruler – A 12" steel ruler gives a straight and accurate edge for tracing straight lines. Large rotary cutting rulers may be too unwieldy and actually cause distortion when tracing.
Masking tape – This not-too-sticky tape will help you keep the paper in place while you are tracing.
Tracing paper – This is used to trace some of the full-size master drawings for the larger blocks.
Sewing machine – For foundation piecing, the most basic sewing machine model is adequate. A straight stitch is all that is necessary.
Iron and pressing mat – Place a table with a pressing pad and iron at right angles to your sewing table on your right side, or set your ironing board up next to you at table height.
Short pins with glass heads – Since they are easy to remove while sewing the seam, short pins with glass heads are ideal for pinning the curved seams. Longer pins take too long to remove during sewing.
Thread – A neutral color, halfway between the colors of your fabrics.
Needle – A universal machine needle, size 12 or 14.
Fabric markers – Whatever will draw a visible, not-too-thick line is fine to draw lines on the fabric. My favorite is a gray quilter's pencil.

Experience Counts!

I made my first patchwork bedspread in 1977 while pregnant with my first child. My inspiration was an advertisement in a Dutch craft magazine offering a kit for a cushion made with very pretty red and cream squares and triangles. At the time, I was a cross-stitch fanatic and a keen crochet fan who also possessed some basic dressmaking skills. So, after studying the photograph of the cushion, I decided to have a go at patchwork.

After cutting a 4" x 4" square of cardboard from the back of a calendar, I gathered together all my cotton (and rayon and polyester and linen!) clothes, thinking I would never fit into them again anyway. Placing the square onto the wrong side of the garments, I drew around the shape with a ball-point pen. If the line was not visible enough, I used a felt tipped pen, nice and clear. Then I cut out the patches adding a seam allowance, arranged them on the floor, and assembled my patchwork in rows.

Phase One of my learning process had started because the pen lines were visible through the front of the patchwork! So the next time I used more suitable markers. And there were a lot of next times. In the following decade I made many patchwork bedspreads, all without knowing about quilts and without ever meeting a fellow quilter. The satisfaction of making "something out of nothing" kept me hooked.

Later when our family moved to another area, I gained access to a library that stocked two (the luxury of it!) quilt books, and the world of quilting opened for me. But I never abandoned my technique of drawing around patches. Unwittingly, I had taught myself a very traditional way of making patchwork.

To take advantage of the speed and accuracy it gives, I use the very modern foundation piecing where it makes sense. But when I've "run out of numbers" and need to add new templates to the design, I go back to the tried and tested practice of pinning and sewing on a line!

I readily admit that I've never fully come to grips with rotary cutting. This has a lot to do with the fact that for most of my "patchwork life," I've had small children around. The rotary cutter seemed like a potentially lethal weapon and I shrank away from buying one. So the method of making exact templates, cutting around them with an "eyeballed" seam allowances, and then pinning and sewing on the line has never seemed laborious to me. On the contrary, when I see some who use rotary cutters struggling to keep their points in the right places, I am happy to have my helpful drawn lines. Many people seem to spend enormous amounts of time and money on gadgets designed to assist them with rotary cutting, only to end up with far from accurate results.

General Instructions

If I can do it, you can do it!

In this chapter you will find descriptions of the methods I use to construct my patchwork with accuracy. After an explanation of the way the patterns are to be used, you are guided through the actual sewing of the blocks.

There are step-by-step foundation piecing instructions for those of you who are new to the technique. They are also a handy reference if you need to brush up on your skills. All this begins with an invaluable collection of tips for frustration-free foundation piecing.

But first…

A cautionary tale

Do you recognize this quilter? While on her twice-weekly pilgrimage to a favorite quilt shop, Avida Piecer spots a new book on the shelves. Attracted by the bright cover, she picks it up, leafs through it, and sees a picture of a quilt she simply must make.

Avida adds the book to her pile of fabrics and other impulse buys. Having stacked her haul on the passenger seat of the car so she can fondle her purchases while waiting at traffic lights, she rushes home. Once there, Avida starts on her new project straight away without bothering to read the general instructions in the book (she is, after all, quite an experienced quiltmaker and has a fair idea of the methods used to construct the design).

Very soon, Avida encounters a slight hitch. She ignores it and continues sewing, confident that she knows how to overcome this small problem.

Not long after, Avida finds herself in trouble, unable to complete the next step in the patchwork process. Then she has a bright idea and looks more closely at her new book, turning to that boring bit describing the techniques used to make the projects. It gradually becomes clear to her that she could have avoided a lot of frustration had she just allowed herself to read through the general instructions.

I know Avida well. I am Avida. We've all been there, done that, and have a half-finished quilt to show for it!

So even if you are familiar with foundation piecing, please read through the following pages to help avoid any problems you might encounter with some of the more complicated blocks.

Tips for happy patchworkers

Patchwork and quilting is a hobby and should therefore be enjoyable and relaxing. If you find yourself treating it as an unpleasant chore, take a step back and ask yourself how you can make it rewarding once again. You may simply need to give yourself time to learn a new technique, an effort that may be tricky initially, but will eventually give much satisfaction. You may need to invest in better tools, or organize your workspace so you are more comfortable.

If you are happy with what you are doing, it will show in your quilts! The following tips

should help you toward frustration-free foundation piecing.

Be organized

Organization enhances enjoyment. Sewing is much more enjoyable if there are no minor irritations to spoil the smooth rhythm of the piecing.

With that in mind, organize yourself with the following items at hand for foundation piecing:
- An accurate tracing to sew on.
- A machine threaded with the proper color and an extra bobbin wound with the same thread.
- An iron and pressing pad to your right, so you will not be tempted to skip pressing the patches while you piece. If you need to get up and walk to the ironing board for every patch, it is just too easy to excuse yourself from that vital step in the process!
- A pile of pre-cut patches on your left.
- A piece of white paper, also on your left, to aid in looking at the lines on the tracing while positioning patches.
- Scissors near the pressing board.
- Seam ripper within easy reach.
- A few pins close at hand.
- Perhaps a radio tuned to your favorite station or the cassette of a book on tape.
- The cordless phone close by.

Spend time on what matters!

Don't waste valuable sewing time fiddling with unimportant things like saving fabric, or precise ¼" seams, or obsessive snipping of threads. Instead, invest a little more time and effort in those areas where it will show and on details that will offer a payback for your pains.

Mark color choice on the tracing

Marking the color on the tracing takes a lot of guesswork out of the process while sewing, thus cutting down on mistakes and the need to unpick. Pattern pieces are very irregular in shape and size, and it is not always easy to identify their position in the color picture once you have started piecing. You will be busy enough following the number order, so it will be a relief to see the color of the patch already indicated on the next number you need to sew.

Don't worry about fabric grainlines

Stitching on subsequent patches will stabilize the pieces as you work. On long, straight pieces, you will automatically have the correct grain line, because you will have pre-cut a straight strip.

Handle with care!

Once the paper has been removed, vulnerable bias edges will be exposed, so it is important not to distort the seam allowances by pulling or pressing. Press when the blocks are completely assembled.

Use neutral thread

Removing the freezer paper can be quite hard on stitching, so make sure that your stitches won't show. Light colored thread tends to show up more than a neutral khaki or beige. The chance of stitches showing on the right side of the work is particularly great on the inset corners of the pots in this book. Many white or cream threads creep through when students have not bothered to change their thread as advised.

Use pieces of a generous size

The most common problem in foundation piecing seems to be an overly-careful attitude some quilters have toward cutting up their fabric. Trying to position too-small pieces of fabric takes a lot of time and often leads to unpicking in the end. Find a happy medium between wasting material and wasting time.

When people watch me demonstrate at shows, quite a number will tell me they have tried foundation piecing but have found it hard to come to grips with the technique. When I question them in an attempt to find out where they slip up, it often becomes evident that they are too sparing with their use of fabric.

Perhaps one of the reasons behind their "economy" is the expense of cotton fabrics. But being too frugal leads to frustration when they cannot get the pieces to fit and are constantly having to unpick their work. My advice to them is to try foundation piecing again with some scraps of old shirts and to cut really large pieces until they are more experienced.

Use a large stitch to baste the patch

When in doubt, select a bigger piece. Or try this trick: When unsure about whether a particular piece of fabric is large enough for the number to be covered, stitch the piece in place with a large basting stitch and press it over to check the fit.

If the patch doesn't quite cover the relevant number, the big stitches are easy enough to unpick, so that you can try again. If it does fit, stitch over the long stitches with a regular stitch, then trim and press as usual.

Sometimes it may be quite obvious that the patch will never be big enough, however carefully it is repositioned. So, set that piece aside for use on a smaller patch elsewhere.

Unpicking

If you have to unpick, use a seam ripper to slash every third or fourth stitch on the fabric side of the work. Do not pull at the stitches on the paper side, as this will cause the paper to crumple and tear, and the drawn line will be lost. Once the stitches have been loosened on the fabric side, pull and remove the ends of those stitches. Then turn to the stitching on the paper side, and you will find that the entire line of stitching can easily be removed by pulling at the ends of the thread.

Trimming seams

Use good, sharp dressmaking scissors to trim the seams. Slip the bottom blade of the open scissors between the paper and the fabric seam. With a nice even cut, trim the seam to about ¼" width.

After sewing a light patch onto a dark patch, you may note that the edge of the underlying dark seam is still visible after trimming the seam. In that case, peel the light-colored seam back and shave an extra sliver off the edge of the dark seam. It is well worth doing this to enhance the look of your finished quilt. There is nothing as ugly as a dark seam showing through the front of the quilt, something usually not noticed until the work is hanging on a wall.

Pre-cut patches

Use cheap fabrics or scraps when you first begin experimenting with foundation piecing. Don't try to pre-cut the patches too precisely and remember that the tracing is a mirror image of the actual fabric picture, so it will be very difficult to pre-cut the exact shape, especially when you are not yet experienced in the method. Cut rectangles that are at least ½" longer and wider than the outer edges of the

General Instructions

patch, and be aware of the outward sloping angles of some of the pattern pieces.

Trouble-free triangles

A row of triangles in a pattern can present unique cutting and sewing challenges. Those who have tried to position a straight piece of fabric into a triangular patch know the frustration of wasted time and fabric. To avoid frustration, do yourself a big favor and make a pre-cutting template.

Simply trace one of the largest triangles in the row onto a piece of paper. Cut out the shape, adding roughly ½" around all traced lines. Use this shape to pre-cut all the triangles in the row.

If the triangles form an arc, the triangles on the outside edge of the arc are larger. To accommodate the different sizes, make separate templates for triangles on the outer and inner edges.

Positioning a motif or striped fabric

Whenever you want a fabric to go onto a particular spot in the tracing, identify the middle of that area with a pencil mark. Stick a pin through the middle of the fabric motif from the wrong side and then stick the pin through the paper at the pencil mark. Pin along the rest of the drawn line and use a basting stitch to secure the piece. When satisfied with the position of the fabric, stitch it in place.

The method

The technique used to construct the patchwork in this book may be quite different from your methods.

The patterns are designed and drawn as one block, then the block is divided into template sections for foundation piecing, and single-piece templates.

The design is treated as a jig-saw puzzle, where the separate paper templates are re-assembled in fabric form. To do this accurately, a seam line is drawn on all fabric pieces with the help of the freezer paper templates. Marks are added to the seam lines where they can help in construction and eliminate confusion.

There seems to be some resistance against drawing lines on fabric, but I hope you will give the method in this book a fair chance.

The piecing techniques described in these pages are recommended because they are quick and easy, with less unpicking and more work satisfaction than with other foundation piecing methods.

How to use patterns in this book

The blocks in this book are all constructed using freezer paper templates. A block without curves may consist of one or more foundation pieced templates. These are called sections A, B, etc. In the blocks that contain curves, the foundation pieced section templates are combined with single piece freezer paper templates, called pieces D, E, etc. Before the block is assembled, all fabric pieces will have been prepared with lines and marks drawn onto the wrong side of the fabric. Setting triangles are prepared the same way.

Making freezer paper templates

In this book, where the patterns are too large to be printed on one page, they have been split. Make a master tracing of the entire pattern piece on plain paper. Match up the pieces at the broken line indicating where the pieces should be joined. It is advisable to have this master pattern so you can make any subsequent tracings easily and accurately. In the case of the THISTLE POT pattern, the flower part (Section A) is printed in four sections. Line up the pattern pieces at the broken lines to make a master tracing of the complete Template A pattern.

Trace the pattern pieces onto the dull side of freezer paper. Transfer all numbers and marks from the pattern. The marks at the edges of patterns will help you line up the pieces when you are ready to assemble the blocks. In some cases, you may find that the marks correspond to seam intersections on the next patch. Whenever you have the slightest doubt, always refer back to the main pattern drawing to find out exactly what fits where. If you forget to transfer the marks, you will really notice their absence, especially on the curved pieces.

Reverse patterns are given in this book so you can trace them onto freezer paper without worrying about making a mirror image.

Cut the freezer paper templates exactly on the outside lines; fabric seam allowances will lie outside these lines.

Piecing the blocks

Identify the pattern pieces given for the block and make the freezer paper templates.

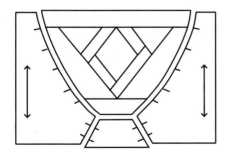

Identify pattern pieces and make templates.

Cut the freezer paper templates exactly on the solid outside lines. Do not cut the numbered templates apart, as these are to be kept whole for foundation piecing. Seam allowances are

added outside of the lines in fabric form only, not on the freezer paper template. Transfer all marks and numbers from the paper tracing onto the freezer paper templates.

Indicate your color choices on the templates with the help of the list given in the block instructions. Remember that the templates show the block in mirror-image, so compare your fabrics to the color illustrations.

Foundation piecing

Assemble the equipment you need, including the numbered freezer paper templates and your fabrics. Pre-cut as advised in "Tips for happy patchworkers" on page 15 and in the block instructions.

You will be sewing on the drawn lines on the dull side of the freezer paper. The fabric picture will appear right side up on the other side, with the wrong side of the fabric sticking to the shiny side of the freezer paper.

Locate #1 on the template. Select a piece of fabric large enough to cover the #1 area plus seam allowances. Iron or pin the wrong side of the fabric to the shiny side of the freezer paper.

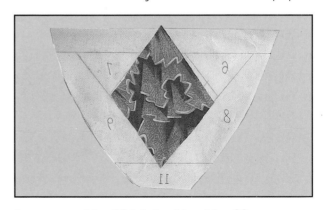

Iron wrong side of fabric to shiny side of freezer paper.

Turn to the drawn side and hold the paper and fabric to a light source to check for adequate seam allowances beyond the lines of #1. Reposition the fabric piece if necessary.

Find #2 on the freezer paper template. Select a piece of fabric large enough to cover #2 plus a generous seam allowance. Place the #2 fabric piece right sides together with the #1 fabric piece. Do not be tempted to align the raw edges of both patches; this has no relevance in this method since you do not have exact seam allowances but roughly cut patches.

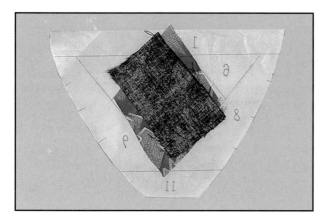

Position second piece right sides together with first.

If you have trouble finding the correct placement, create a mock-up of how the two patches will appear together in the block once they have been sewn. This will give you an angle on which way to turn fabric piece #2 to lie on piece #1.

Keep a white sheet of paper next to your sewing machine and use it as a background to help you position the fabric onto the undrawn side. You will find that you can peek through the freezer paper template and see the lines far more clearly with the help of the light background.

You will be sewing on the line between #1 and #2 on the drawn side of the template. Check that you have placed the fabric patch correctly

to catch this line. Make sure also that the fabric will cover the entire area of #2 on the template after sewing and pressing over, with seam allowances beyond the drawn lines for the patch. Once you are happy about the placement, put in some pins to hold fabric and paper together.

Turn to the drawn side and sew on the line between areas #1 and #2 through all layers – paper and fabrics pieces #1 and #2.

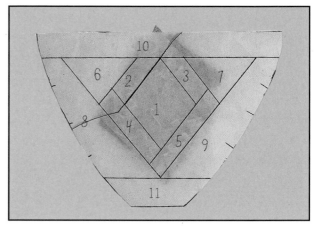

Sew on the line between #1 and #2.

Sew with a slightly shorter stitch than usual and start and finish four or five stitches beyond either end of the line. Trim the seam and press fabric piece #2 over the shiny paper patch #2.

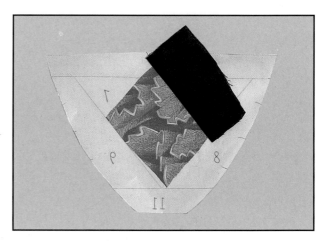

Press fabric #2 over shiny paper #2.

Continue with #3 and subsequent numbers in the same way.

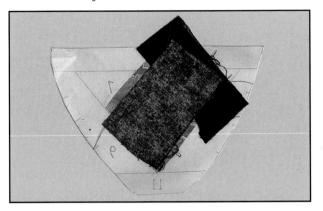

Continue adding fabric pieces in numerical order.

Identify the next sewing line by finding the next patch in numerical order. Then find the line that lies between that patch and the numbers already sewn; stitch on that line.

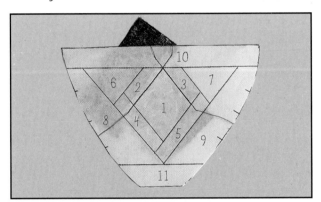

Stitch on lines between sequential numbers.

Make sure you leave a generous seam allowance around the outside edge of the template.

Leave a generous seam allowance.

You will become more confident with experience, and as long as you use fabric patches of generous size, you will soon settle into a steady piecing rhythm. Beware of any very irregular shapes on the tracing and make absolutely sure that your patches are large enough to cover any outward angles of the shape.

When you stitch the patches bordering the outside edge of the template, stitch well into the seam allowance, so you can be confident that those stitches won't unravel when you remove the paper at the end of the piecing sequence. I cannot count the number of times a little "remedial" work was necessary when this advice was not followed.

After piecing all the numbers, draw a seam line around the edge of the freezer paper on the wrong side of the fabric, transferring all the marks onto the fabric.

Remove the paper carefully. Begin at the outer edges by pinching the stitching in the fabric seam allowance firmly between finger and thumb and then working the paper loose. Using this method will lessen the chance of unraveling stitches. When the paper is removed, the completed section is ready to sew to the rest of the block.

After a foundation piecing session, remove the sewing machine needle you have used from your machine and put it in a separate holder. It will only be fit to use for your next foundation piecing project, since sewing through paper will have made it too blunt for normal use.

Piecing blocks without curves

Five blocks in this book have no curved pieces. They are TULIP POT, POT BLOOM, IRIS POT, FLOWERCLUB, and KALEIDOPOT. Foundation piece the sections for each part. Use a ruler and a fabric marker to draw exact seam lines around the edge of the freezer paper template on the wrong side of the fabric. Transfer all the marks onto the fabric.

Remove the freezer paper carefully. Assemble the block sections by pinning and sewing on the drawn lines, matching the marks.

Piecing blocks with curves

Four blocks in this book have curved pieces that require slightly different piecing techniques. Included are CACTUS POT, DAISY POT, THISTLE POT, and POT NOODLE.

Identify the sections for foundation piecing templates, trace them onto freezer paper, and foundation piece them. Iron the remaining single piece templates onto the wrong side of the relevant fabrics, taking care to follow any directions regarding grainlines.

Cut out the pieces with a generous seam allowance (approximately ½ inch). The seam allowance need not be exact, as it is simply there to help you pin the patches together.

On all fabric pieces, draw exact seam lines around the edge of the freezer paper onto the

Draw seam lines on fabric.

wrong side of the fabric and transfer all marks. Remove the paper.

Following the instructions for the project, lay out all the fabric pieces, wrong side up, for the block or part-block. Check to be certain all lines and marks have been drawn on the fabric. Make sure all paper is removed.

Assemble patches in the order given in the instructions. Pick up the relevant patches and first pin the corners to the foundation at each end. Bring the marks (or marks and seam intersections) together and pin through these.

Then pin between the marks. If the seam is curved, ease the edges so the lines lie together, pinning securely and placing the pins perpendicular to the seam. Use as many pins as necessary to achieve a seam that curves without gaps and bulges.

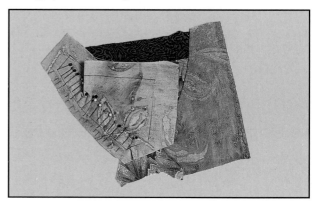

Ease and pin edges.

If you have pinned correctly, you should now be able to sew this seam without mishaps. Those of you brave enough to sew over pins, may feel free to do so. I'm too scared of flying bits of metal to attempt this, so I sew carefully on the line, removing pins just before the needle reaches them. Hold the pinned seam firmly between finger and thumb while stitching to make sure your painstaking pinning work does not dislodge.

The time spent on pinning is amply compensated by the time saved not having to unpick seams after sewing.

Trim the seam. Press the block gently when all the pieces have been sewn. You will find there is no need to clip curves in the blocks shown in this book. Just let the seams lie in their chosen direction and the block will lie flat.

Piecing pot parts with curves
The pot sections of four blocks in this book contain curves and require special attention. They are THISTLE POT, DAISY POT, CACTUS POT, and POT NOODLE.

The background patches at the sides of the pots are set-in pieces. If you have ever pieced an eight-pointed star, you will be familiar with this technique. For a set-in piece to sit happily within the patchwork, it is essential that seam allowances on the surrounding pieces not be stitched down. To accommodate the set-in patch, they must be free to lie in any direction.

Assembling pots with curved pieces
The following directions will help you sew the curved pots of THISTLE POT, CACTUS POT, POT NOODLE, and DAISY POT.

Position sections and curved pieces.

Sew the pedestal to the bottom of the curved pot. Stitch only on the line, do not stitch into the seam allowances at either end, but secure

beginning and end stitching exactly at the start and finish of the drawn line.

Set in the curved pieces. Follow the instructions for curved piecing and sew them to the sides of the pot, taking care not to stitch into the seam allowance at the point where the three pieces meet. Secure the stitching at this point.

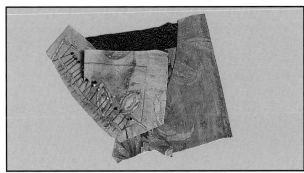

Attach curved pieces to section.

Sew the short bottom ends of the curved pieces to the pot pedestal, matching marks and again securing the stitching at the point where the three meet. Trim seams.

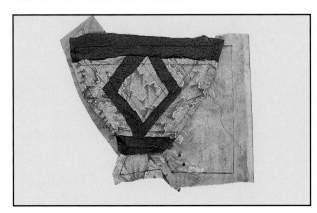

Attach bottom seams of curved pieces.

Joining the blocks
Use the drawn line at the outside edge of the blocks to pin and sew the blocks together. To sew the setting triangles onto the blocks, pin and sew on the lines that you have drawn on the blocks and on the fabric triangles. Trim seams.

Happy Sewing!

Pot Luck Sampler

POT LUCK SAMPLER
45" x 48"

Dutch Flower Pot Quilts – Anja Townrow

POT LUCK SAMPLER is made using the first seven blocks in this book.

To give unity to the design, the same light green marbled fabric was used as the background of all the blocks. For the rest of the colors in the flower pots, a mixture of scrap fabrics were chosen, keeping to a palette of green, pink, purple, red, orange, and yellow.

Once the flower pots were made, the setting fabrics were selected. For these, five different prints were used that picked up some of the colors in the blocks without being too overpowering. The dark green inner border seemed to frame the blocks well, and the wide brown/yellow checked border was a lucky find for the perfect finishing touch. The dark green is picked up again in the binding.

The quilt was layered with cotton batting and a bargain-buy cotton print. Then invisible thread was used for stitch-in-the-ditch quilting around every flower pot and around the block settings.

Having thus secured the layers, free-hand flowers and leaves were quilted in the light green background, using a fine matching thread. A variety of programmed stitches in a red/gold metallic thread play around in the pots and flowers. The same thread was used to quilt free-hand shapes in the setting triangles and to quilt parallel lines in the borders.

To make POT LUCK SAMPLER

Piece the blocks for the sampler, and add corner pieces. For TULIP POT and CACTUS POT blocks, add borders to obtain a finished measurement of 14½" x 15", excluding seam allowances. Lay out all blocks as shown in the placement diagram on page 26. Assemble the blocks into vertical rows, then join the rows.

Add the borders. The finished width of the green inner border is 1", and the checked border is 3" wide.

POT LUCK SAMPLER
Fabric and material requirements

Amount	Fabric
1 yard	Light green
Fat quarters or a selection of scraps	Pink, purple, fuchsia, red, yellow, orange, and at least six greens
Fat quarters	At least five patterned fabrics for the settings
1 yard	Dark green
1 yard	Brown/yellow check
53" x 50"	Batting and backing
Other materials	Invisible thread Decorative thread

The label

To quickly make a label that perfectly matched the quilt in color and style, one of the easier block patterns without curves was chosen for a label. The pattern was reduced by 50% on a photocopier, then traced and foundation pieced as usual, using fabric scraps from POT LUCK SAMPLER. The block was lined and borders added before sewing details about the quilt (name, maker, year) onto the label with the help of programmed stitches.

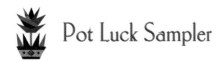
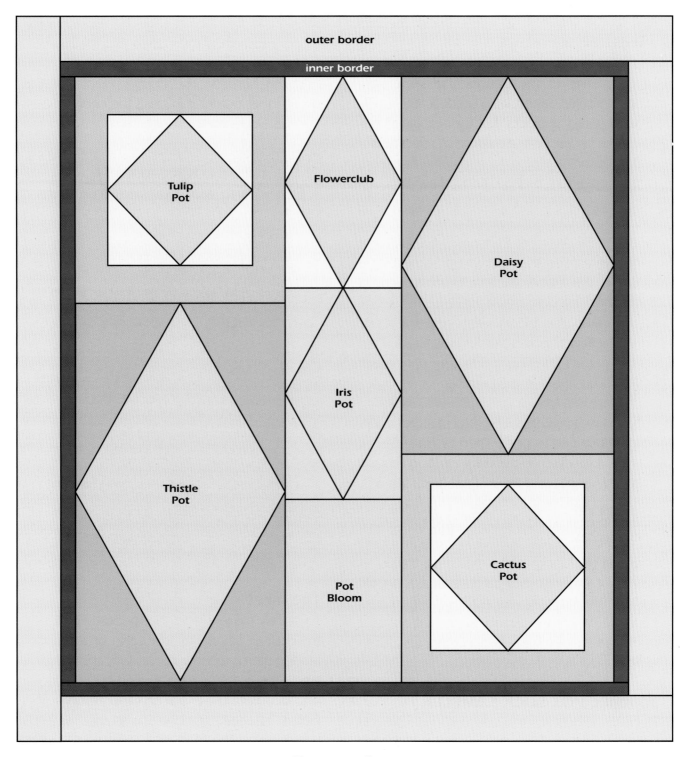

Placement diagram.

Tulip Pot

Block Size 7" x 7"

Without a doubt, this is the easiest and quickest block in this book. The entire block is foundation-pieced as a whole, so that on completion of all 20 numbers, your block is ready to be used in a quilt. Add four corner triangles and borders to set the block into POT LUCK SAMPLER.

Tulip Pot

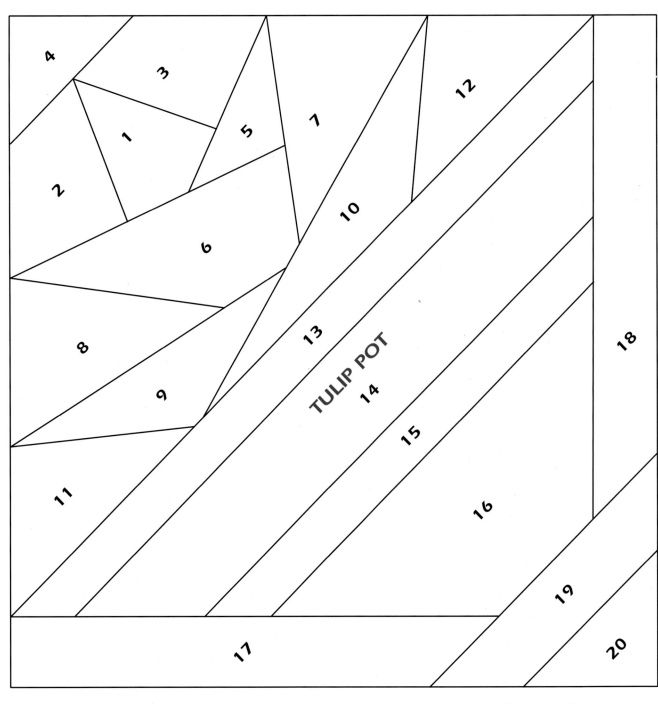

Add generous seam allowances (¼" to ½") to all fabric pieces when cutting.

TULIP POT
Color Selection

Piece	Color
2, 3, 4, 7, 8, 11,12, 17, 18, 20	Light green
1, 14	Yellow
5	Pink
6	Red
9	Medium green
10	Dark green
13, 15, 19	Purple
16	Fuchsia

TULIP HARVEST
24" x 24"

Five blocks are set with triangles to form a star design. For the setting triangles, use the template pattern on page 30. Autumn colors and a creamy background combine to make this a very attractive quilt. Note how the bottom bars on the pots work together to give movement to this setting.

Tulip Pot Variations

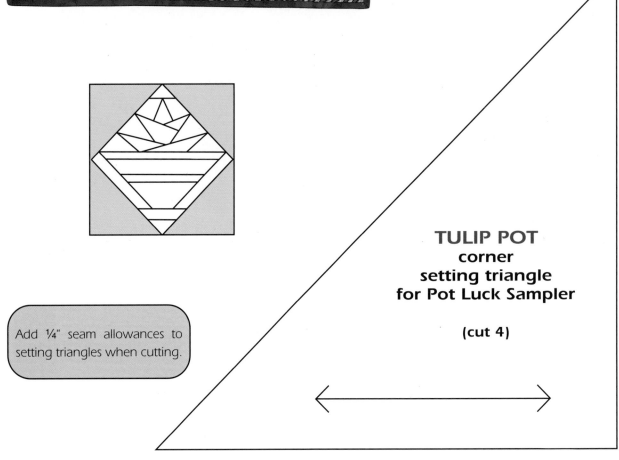

TULIP JAZZ
20" x 20"

Choose a dramatic deep blue, enlivened with very bright pink and greens for a modern look. When four blocks are joined to form a square, the lower bars in the pots create a new design that gives definition to the center of the quilt.

TULIP POT
corner
setting triangle
for Pot Luck Sampler

(cut 4)

Add ¼" seam allowances to setting triangles when cutting.

ORIENTAL TULIPS
20" x 20"

A lovely Japanese-style floral print was the basis of the color scheme in this quilt. The green used for the background is quite strong, but blends in well with the abundant flowers.

Tulip Pot
Variations

TRADITIONAL TULIPS
24" x 24"

An almost antique look is achieved here by quiltmaker Jackie Tonks, who likes using subdued colors and small prints. The triangle border makes a graceful frame for the quilt.

Flowerclub

Block Size 8" x 14"

This flower block is simple to make and looks good in any setting. Ideal for using up your scraps, this design is a classic favorite. Add setting triangles, C and Cr, page 36, to use this block in POT LUCK SAMPLER.

Add generous seam allowances (¼" to ½") to all fabric pieces when cutting.

FLOWERCLUB
Color Selection
Section A

Piece	Color
2, 3, 4, 8, 9, 12, 13	Light green
1	Deep purple
5	Red
6	Fuchsia
7	Yellow
10	Mid-green
11	Bright green

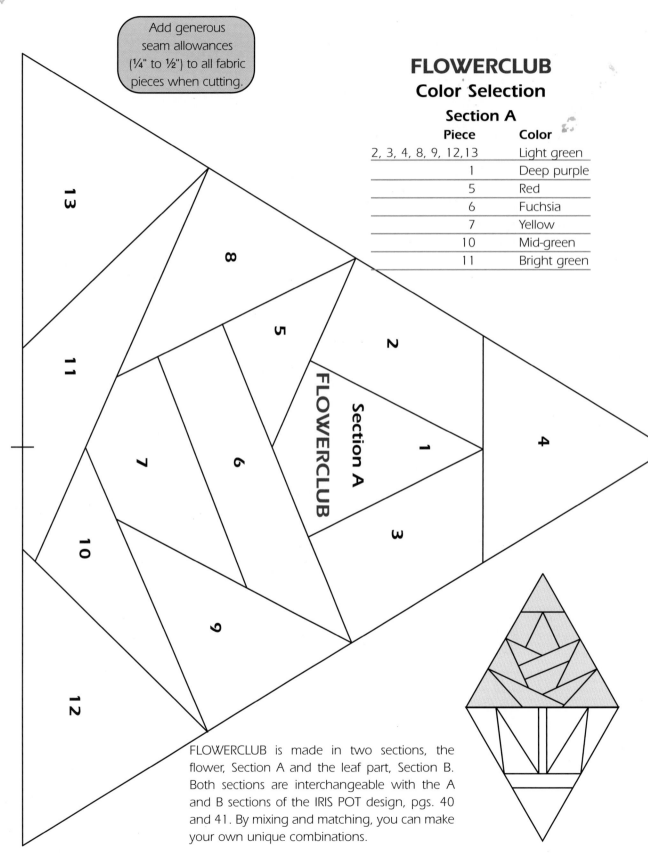

Section A — FLOWERCLUB

FLOWERCLUB is made in two sections, the flower, Section A and the leaf part, Section B. Both sections are interchangeable with the A and B sections of the IRIS POT design, pgs. 40 and 41. By mixing and matching, you can make your own unique combinations.

FLOWERCLUB
Color Selection
Section B

Piece	Color
2, 3, 6, 7, 9	Light green
1, 4, 5, 8	Dark green

Add generous seam allowances (¼" to ½") to all fabric pieces when cutting.

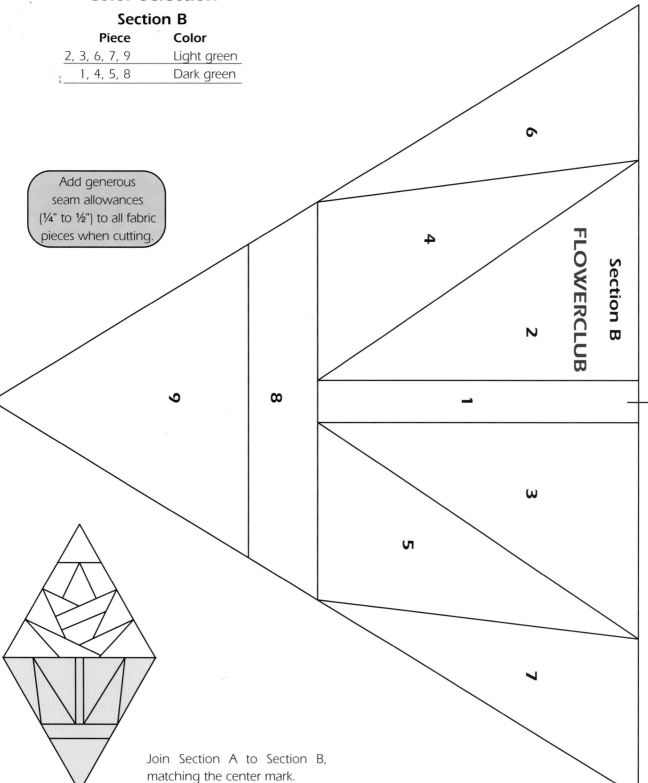

Section B
FLOWERCLUB

Join Section A to Section B, matching the center mark.

Flowerclub

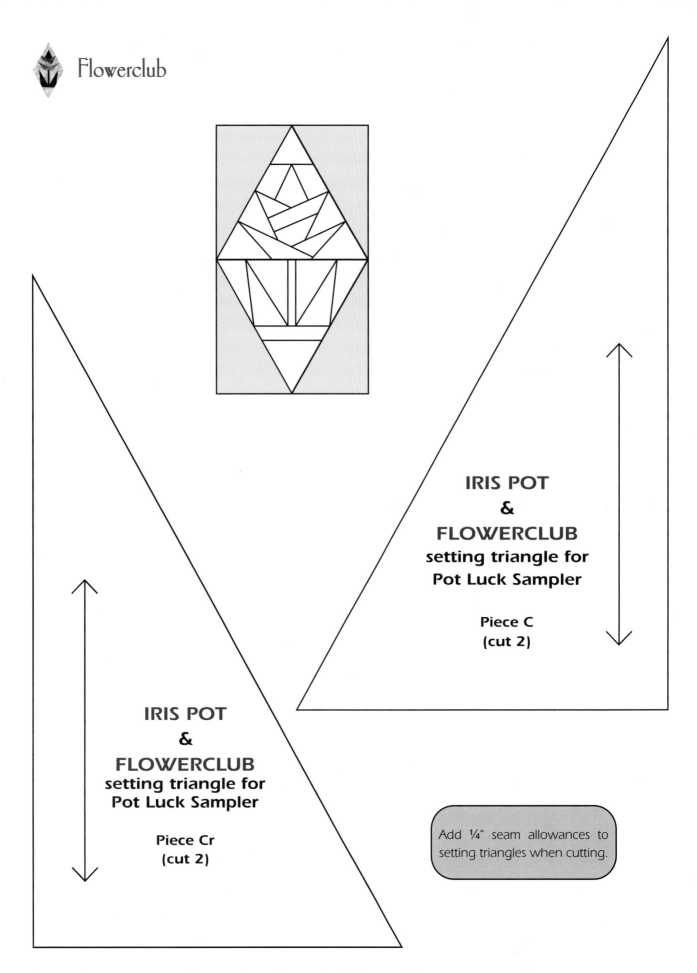

IRIS POT
&
FLOWERCLUB
setting triangle for
Pot Luck Sampler

Piece C
(cut 2)

IRIS POT
&
FLOWERCLUB
setting triangle for
Pot Luck Sampler

Piece Cr
(cut 2)

Add ¼" seam allowances to setting triangles when cutting.

Dutch Flower Pot Quilts – Anja Townrow

CHRISTMAS FLOWERS

32" x 28"

Jackie Tonks achieved a totally different look by using Christmas fabric scraps to sew this beautiful quilt.

Note: The setting patches for the quilts shown here can be made by using Section A and B templates and the setting corner pieces C and Cr. For the corners of FLORIENTAL, combine FLOWERCLUB Section A with FLOWERCLUB pieces C and Cr to form the correct shape.

FLOWER ART

32" x 28"

The patterned fabric in the setting diamonds was the inspiration for this quilt. Strong colors for the flowers and an appliquéd motif add impact.

Flowerclub Variations

FLORIENTAL
16" x 28"

Four blocks made with colorful scraps form a large diamond. The fabric used in the setting corners gives an Oriental flavor to this wallhanging.

CATS IN THE FLOWERPATCH
24" x 14"

Cats sun themselves among greenery in the setting patches around the three scrappy Flowerclub blocks. A longer row of blocks would make an attractive table runner.

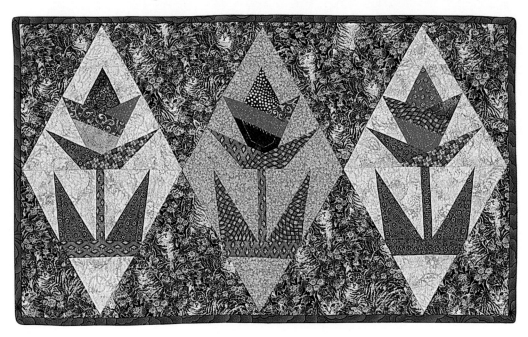

Iris Pot

Block Size 8" x 14"

This Flower Pot pattern is a stylized interpretation of an Iris in its furled stage.
The block is foundation pieced in two sections, A and B. Each section is an
equilateral triangle, and when joined, the two form a diamond.

Iris Pot

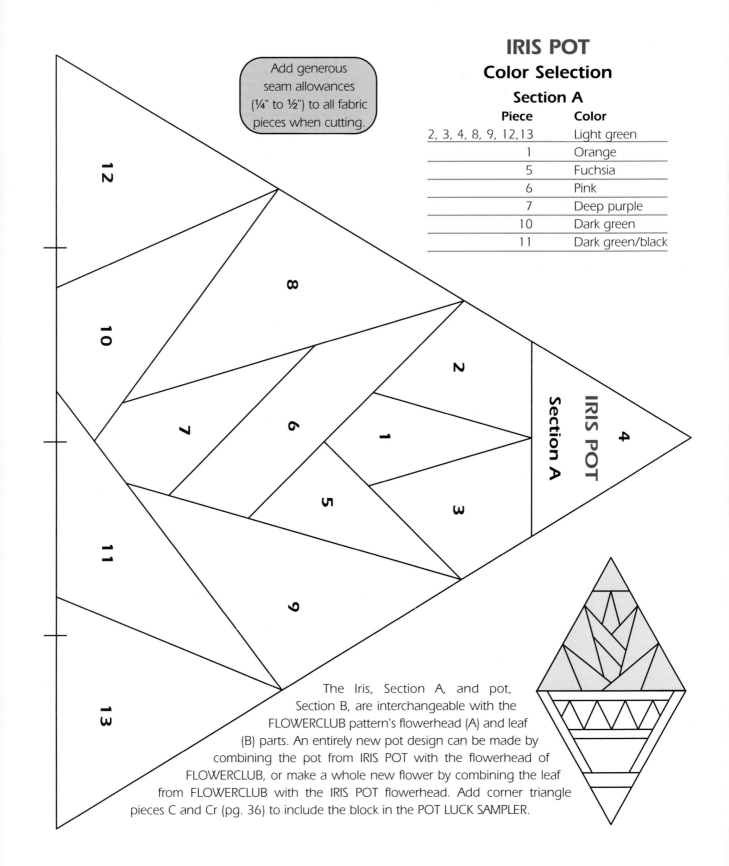

Add generous seam allowances (¼" to ½") to all fabric pieces when cutting.

IRIS POT
Color Selection
Section A

Piece	Color
2, 3, 4, 8, 9, 12, 13	Light green
1	Orange
5	Fuchsia
6	Pink
7	Deep purple
10	Dark green
11	Dark green/black

IRIS POT

Section A

The Iris, Section A, and pot, Section B, are interchangeable with the FLOWERCLUB pattern's flowerhead (A) and leaf (B) parts. An entirely new pot design can be made by combining the pot from IRIS POT with the flowerhead of FLOWERCLUB, or make a whole new flower by combining the leaf from FLOWERCLUB with the IRIS POT flowerhead. Add corner triangle pieces C and Cr (pg. 36) to include the block in the POT LUCK SAMPLER.

IRIS POT
Color Selection
Section B

Piece	Color
13, 14, 16	Light green
2, 3, 6, 7	Yellow
1, 4, 5, 8, 9, 15	Deep purple
10, 11	Red
12	Fuchsia

Add generous seam allowances (¼" to ½") to all fabric pieces when cutting.

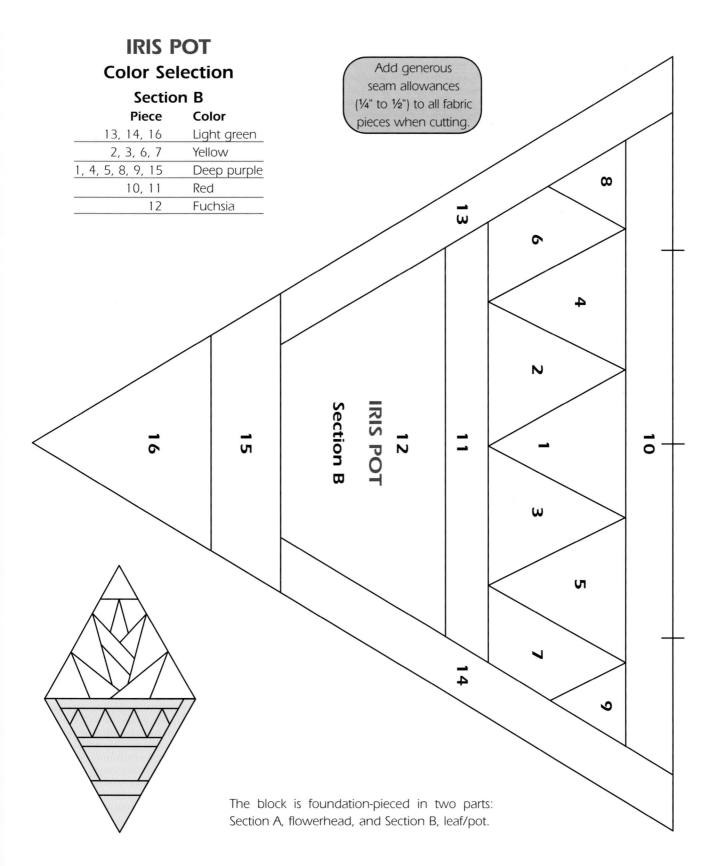

The block is foundation-pieced in two parts: Section A, flowerhead, and Section B, leaf/pot.

SPOT THE POTS

32" x 28"

Six diamonds formed by sections A and B, set with six spotted diamonds, make this striking quilt.
The triangles in the pots make their own distinctive pattern in this kaleidoscopic setting.

FIESTA
32" x 28"

The setting diamonds in this quilt have been cut from a brightly striped fabric to showcase both the fabric and the shape of the quilt. A dark background in the Iris block makes the flowers more prominent. Again, yellow triangles in the pot form a new design "in the round." An appliquéd spiral motif adds even more movement to this quilt.

Pot Bloom

Block Size 8" x 12"

Big and blowsy, this bloom almost bursts out of its pot. The exuberant flowerhead gives lots of scope for varied use of color. This will be a very useful block for a pattern collection. Adding sashes and borders will make a bed quilt with just 25 blocks. Four or five blocks in a row form an interesting wallhanging above a bed. A single block with borders makes a quick cushion or bag.

SUNNY BLOOMS
30" x 16"

Three identical POT BLOOMS are set with a bright patterned border. The gray background fabric was chosen to resemble a window pane. Checked fabric in the top and bottom strips enhances the look of the pot.

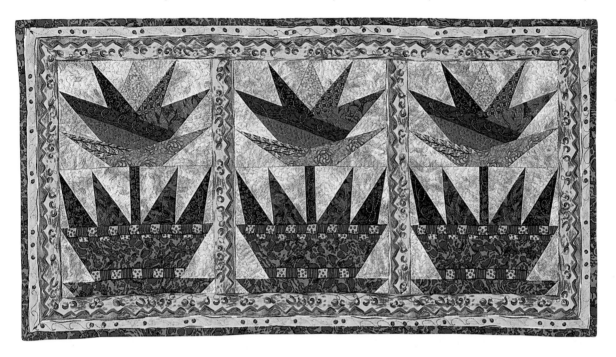

MIXED BLOOMS
30" x 16"

Jackie Tonks used a lot of scraps for the flowerheads to give each bloom its own color scheme in this quilt. Although Jackie used identical fabrics for her pots, she added variation by quilting a different design in each one.

POT BLOOM
Color Selection
Section A

Piece	Color		
2, 3, 6, 7, 11, 12, 15, 16	Light green	8	Red
1	Yellow	9	Pink
4	Purple	10	Deep purple
5	Orange	13	Bright green
		14	Medium green

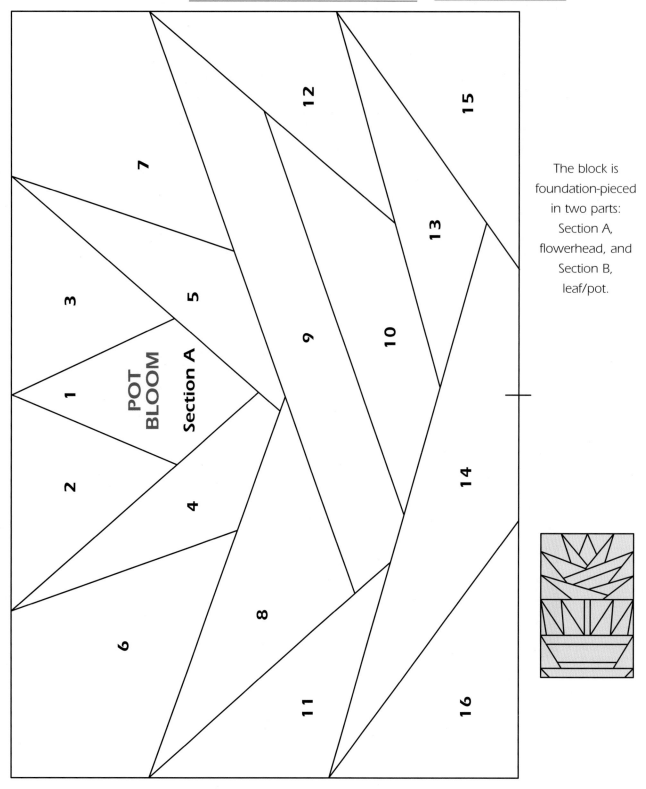

The block is foundation-pieced in two parts: Section A, flowerhead, and Section B, leaf/pot.

POT BLOOM
Color Selection
Section B

Piece	Color		
2, 3, 6, 7, 10, 11, 15, 16, 18, 19	Light green	12, 14	Yellow
1, 4, 5	Medium green	13	Pink
8, 9	Dark green	17	Deep purple

Add generous seam allowances (¼" to ½") to all fabric pieces when cutting.

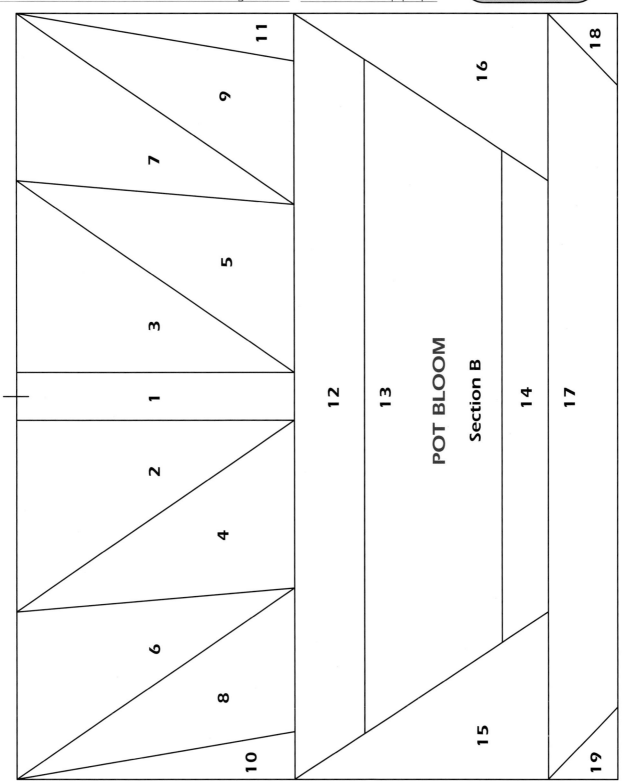

Pot Bloom Variation

LASTING GIFT

12" x 16"

This is a quick Mothers' Day present that will last a lot longer than any floral tribute. The diamond shapes are appliquéd to the pot to add extra interest, while the striped border gives movement to this small wallhanging.

Thistle Pot

Block Size 14½" x 25"

Since the curves that shape the pot are very gentle and easy to sew, this an excellent project for a first try at curved piecing. The block is made in two parts that combine foundation piecing with curved piecing: a foundation pieced flower part, Section A; and a pot part that includes Section B, C and pieces, D and Dr.

THISTLE POT
Color Selection

Section A

Piece	Color
2, 3, 6, 7, 10, 11, 14, 15, 18, 19, 20	Light green
1 (4" x 3")	Yellow
4 (5" x 3")	Orange
5 (4" x 7")	Red
8 (6" x 3")	Deep purple
9 (8" x 4")	Fuchsia
12 (3" x 7")	Olive green
13 (10" x 4")	Medium green
16 (4" x 9")	Sage green
17 (9" x 4")	Dark green

THISTLE POT is the same size diamond as DAISY POT, so the settings for both blocks are interchangeable.

Add the corners K and Kr (pgs. 74 and 75) to include the block in the POT LUCK SAMPLER.

Make a copy of pattern pieces by tracing or using a non-distorting photocopier. Join pattern sections on dashed lines as indicated. Make a full-sized master copy of the entire pattern before tracing pattern pieces onto the dull side of freezer paper.

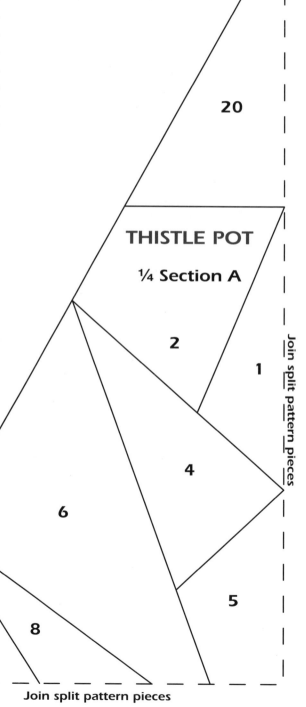

Add generous seam allowances (¼" to ½") to all fabric pieces when cutting.

THISTLE POT

¼ Section A

Join split pattern pieces

Join split pattern pieces

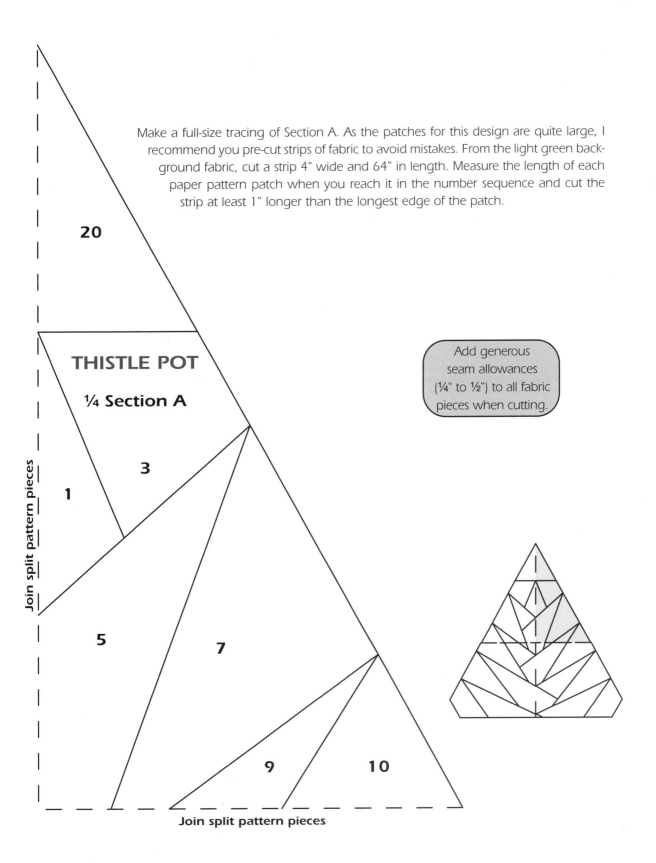

Make a full-size tracing of Section A. As the patches for this design are quite large, I recommend you pre-cut strips of fabric to avoid mistakes. From the light green background fabric, cut a strip 4" wide and 64" in length. Measure the length of each paper pattern patch when you reach it in the number sequence and cut the strip at least 1" longer than the longest edge of the patch.

20

THISTLE POT

¼ Section A

Join split pattern pieces

1

3

5

7

9

10

Add generous seam allowances (¼" to ½") to all fabric pieces when cutting.

Join split pattern pieces

Make a copy of pattern pieces by tracing or using a non-distorting photocopier.
Join pattern sections on dashed lines as indicated. Make a full-sized master copy of
the entire pattern before tracing pattern pieces onto the dull side of freezer paper.

Add generous
seam allowances
(¼" to ½") to all fabric
pieces when cutting.

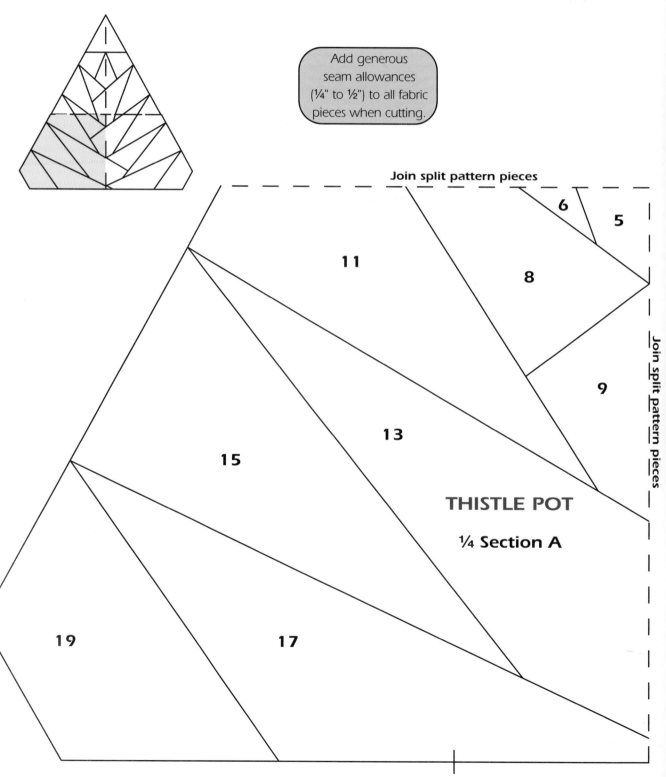

Join split pattern pieces

6

5

11

8

9

Join split pattern pieces

13

15

THISTLE POT

¼ Section A

19

17

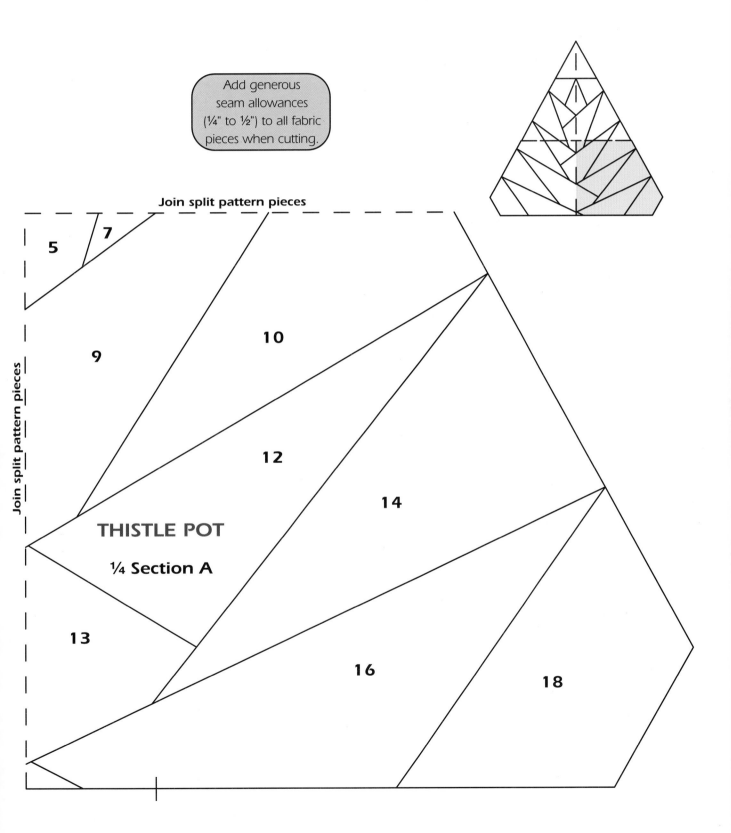

Add generous seam allowances (¼" to ½") to all fabric pieces when cutting.

Join split pattern pieces

5
7
9
10
12
14

Join split pattern pieces

THISTLE POT

¼ Section A

13
16
18

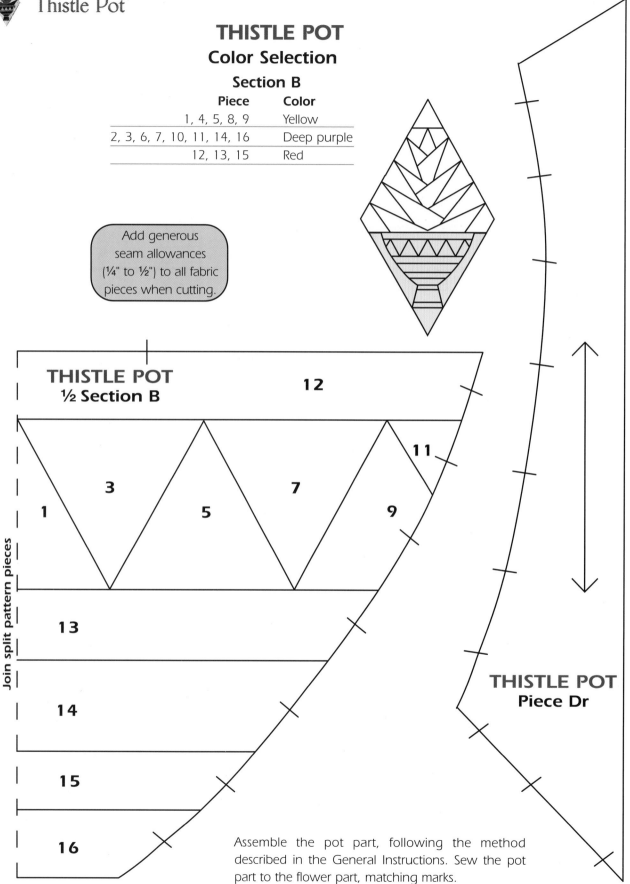

THISTLE POT
Color Selection
Section B

Piece	Color
1, 4, 5, 8, 9	Yellow
2, 3, 6, 7, 10, 11, 14, 16	Deep purple
12, 13, 15	Red

Add generous seam allowances (¼" to ½") to all fabric pieces when cutting.

THISTLE POT
½ Section B

12

11

3

7

1

5

9

Join split pattern pieces

13

14

15

16

THISTLE POT
Piece Dr

Assemble the pot part, following the method described in the General Instructions. Sew the pot part to the flower part, matching marks.

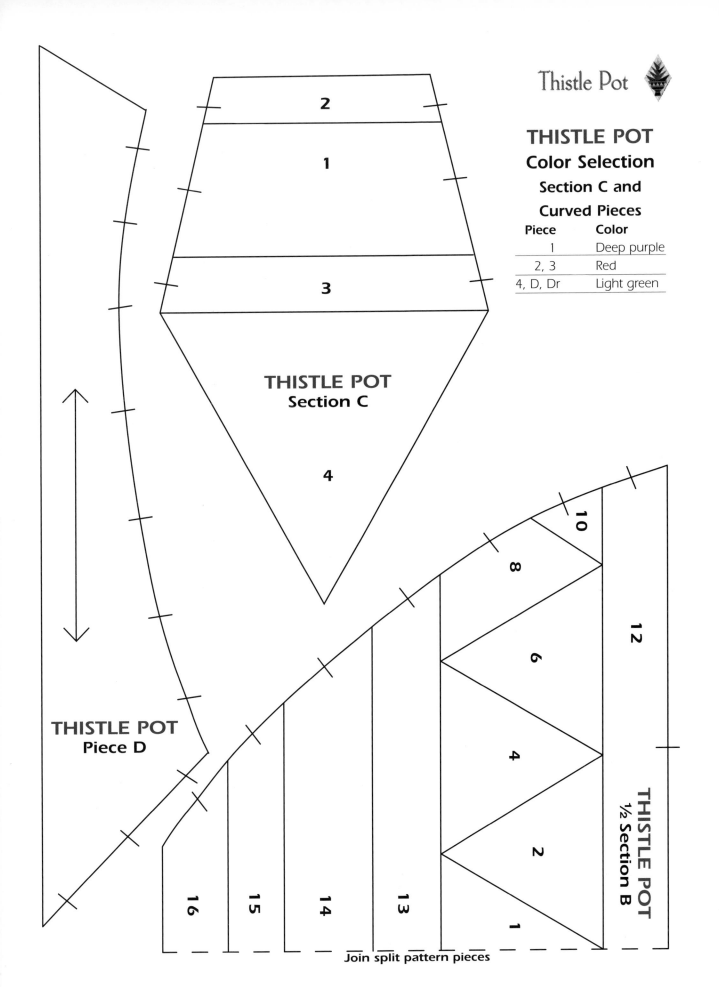

Thistle Pot

THISTLE POT
Color Selection
Section C and
Curved Pieces

Piece	Color
1	Deep purple
2, 3	Red
4, D, Dr	Light green

THISTLE POT
Section C

THISTLE POT
Piece D

THISTLE POT
½ Section B

Join split pattern pieces

TRELLIS THISTLE
23½" x 34"

This setting is easily achieved by dividing the corner templates K and Kr (p59gs. 74 and 75) with parallel lines. Trace and foundation piece. Add mitered borders. Careful color placement will result in the airy trellis effect.

PAINTED THISTLE
14½" x 25"

The blue/green corners pick up the blue from the pot and the green of
the leaves. The quilting, done by Jackie Tonks in a wide variety of threads,
stitches, and freehand techniques, makes this small quilt really special.

Cactus Pot

Block Size 8" x 8"

Simple foundation piecing combined with two gentle curves make this plump little flower pot
a lovely addition to your block library.

The block is made in two parts: the flower part, Section A, and the pot part, Sections B, D, and pieces C and Cr. Set the block with corner triangles, E and Er, and add borders to include CACTUS POT in the POT LUCK SAMPLER.

Add generous seam allowances (¼" to ½") to all fabric pieces when cutting.

CACTUS POT
Color Selection
Section A

Piece	Color
2, 3, 6, 7, 10, 11, 14, 15, 16	Light green
1	Pink
4	Red
5	Aubergine
8	Medium purple
29	Fuchsia
12	Bright green
13	Medium green

Join split pattern pieces

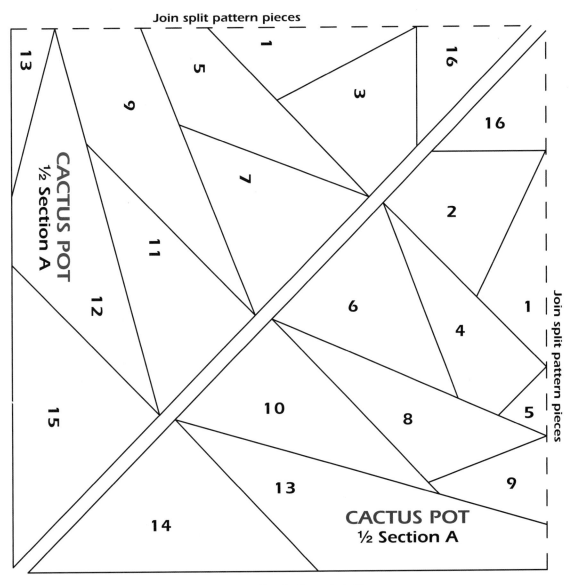

CACTUS POT ½ Section A

Join split pattern pieces

CACTUS POT ½ Section A

 Cactus Pot

CACTUS POT
Color Selection
Section B

Piece	Color
1, 4, 5	Red
2, 3, 6, 7	Yellow
8, 9	Deep purple
C, Cr	Light green

Add generous seam allowances (¼" to ½") to all fabric pieces when cutting.

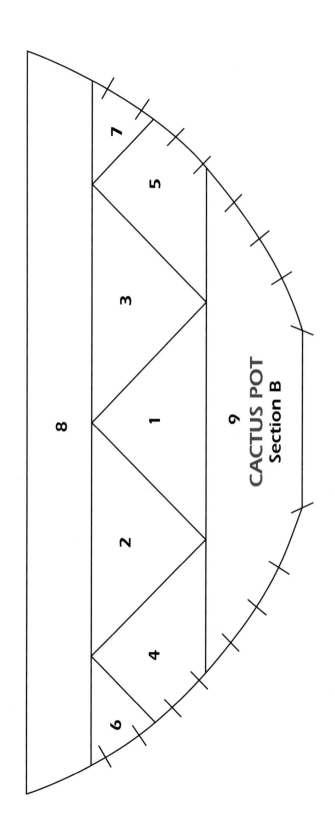

CACTUS POT
Section B

CACTUS POT
Color Selection
Section D

Piece	Color
1	Deep purple
2	Light green

Foundation piece the sections, and assemble the pot part following the method described in the General Instructions. Join the flower section to the pot section.

Add generous seam allowances (¼" to ½") to all fabric pieces when cutting.

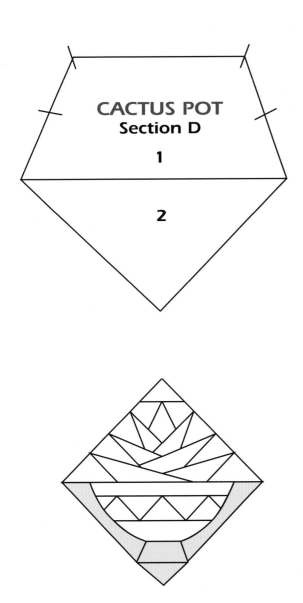

CACTUS POT
Section D

1

2

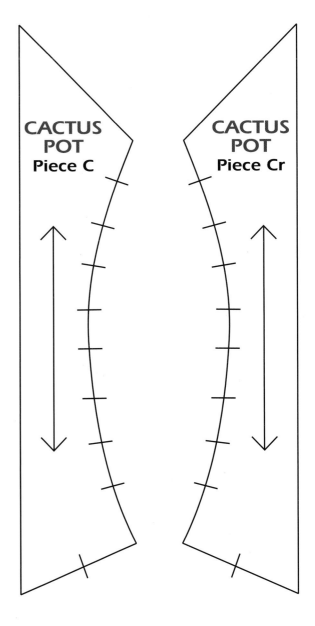

CACTUS POT
Piece C

CACTUS POT
Piece Cr

 Cactus Pot

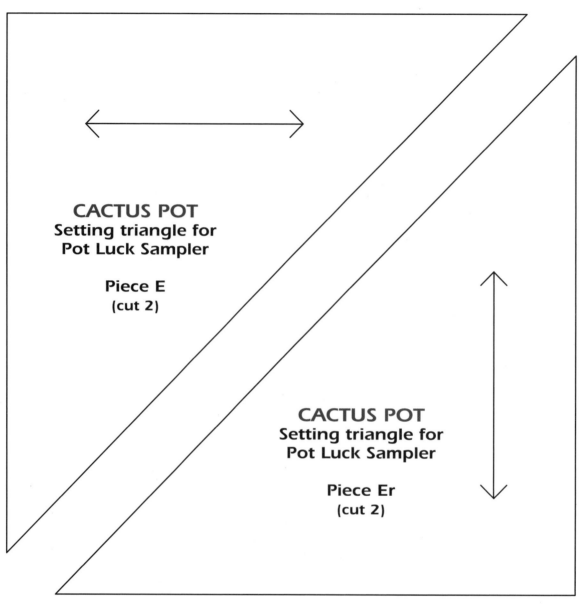

CACTUS POT
Setting triangle for Pot Luck Sampler

Piece E
(cut 2)

CACTUS POT
Setting triangle for Pot Luck Sampler

Piece Er
(cut 2)

Add ¼" seam allowances to setting triangles when cutting.

GOUDA CACTUS
24" x 24"

The colors in this quilt reflect the glowing, deep glaze of "Gouds Plateel," the clay pottery ware produced in the Dutch town of Gouda.

Cactus Pot Variations

BLUE CACTUS
24" x 24"

Made by Jackie Tonks from blue, white, and green scraps, this quilt clearly shows it is not necessary to plan your color scheme too far ahead. The dark green setting square and triangles pull the blocks together. For the quilting in the center square, Jackie simply stitched through a tracing of the entire CACTUS POT block.

SEA CACTUS
24" x 24"

Join four CACTUS POT blocks to form a square, set on point. Set half blocks with borders to form the corner triangles, and the result is this striking design. The appliquéd motif adds an essential focus to the middle of the quilt.

Daisy Pot

Block Size 14½" x 25"

It can be argued that this block is the prettiest in this collection, but it is also the most challenging to sew. However, by being methodical and concentrating on the correct order of construction, you'll find the result to be well worth the effort!

Dutch Flower Pot Quilts – Anja Townrow

DAISY POT and THISTLE POT are both diamonds of the same size, so the settings and quilt ideas for either block are interchangeable. Add two K and Kr corner triangles to use the block in the POT LUCK SAMPLER.

DAISY POT is made in two halves: a flowerhead triangle consisting of piece A and Sections B, C, and E; and a pot and leaf triangle comprising Sections F, G, H, I, and pieces J and Jr.

Flowerhead Assembly

To make the flowerhead triangle, make full-size templates A and B. Foundation piece B, C, and E. Cut piece A. Appliqué piece D using method shown on page 70.

Assemble the flowerhead as shown in Flowerhead Assembly Diagram. Sew B to C, matching seams. Sew A to BC, matching marks; sew E to ABC.

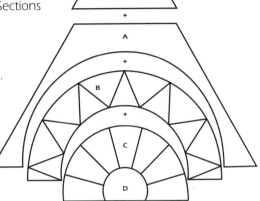

Flowerhead Assembly Diagram

DAISY POT
Color Selection

Section E

Piece	Color
1, 4	Light green
2	Medium green
3	Yellow

Add generous seam allowances (¼" to ½") to all fabric pieces when cutting.

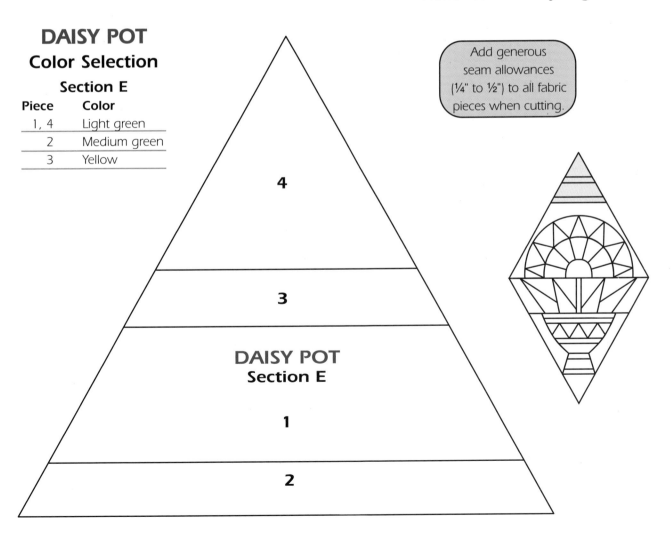

DAISY POT
Section E

4

3

1

2

Daisy Pot

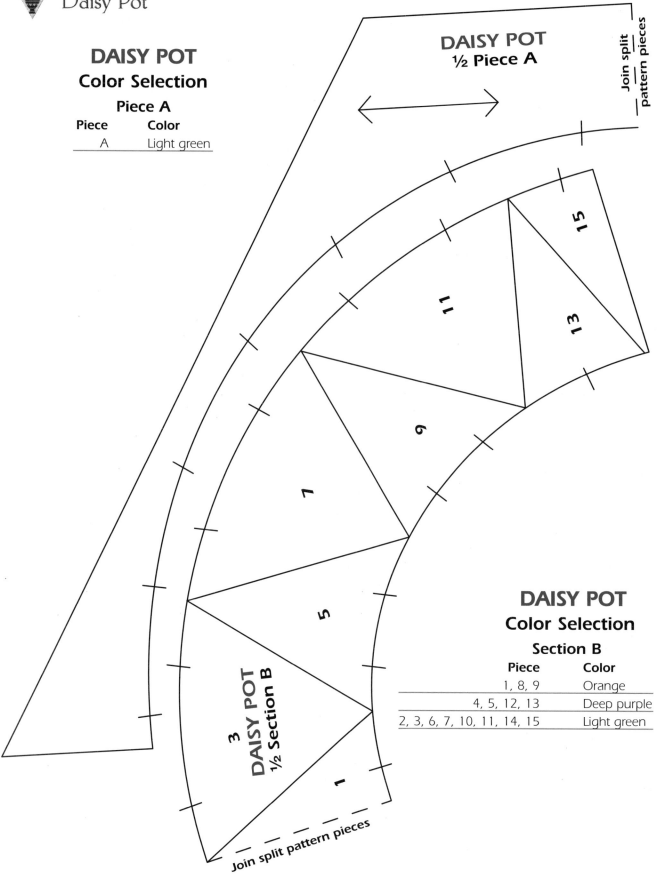

DAISY POT
Color Selection
Piece A

Piece	Color
A	Light green

DAISY POT
½ Piece A

Join split pattern pieces

15

11

13

6

7

5

3
DAISY POT
½ Section B

1

Join split pattern pieces

DAISY POT
Color Selection
Section B

Piece	Color
1, 8, 9	Orange
4, 5, 12, 13	Deep purple
2, 3, 6, 7, 10, 11, 14, 15	Light green

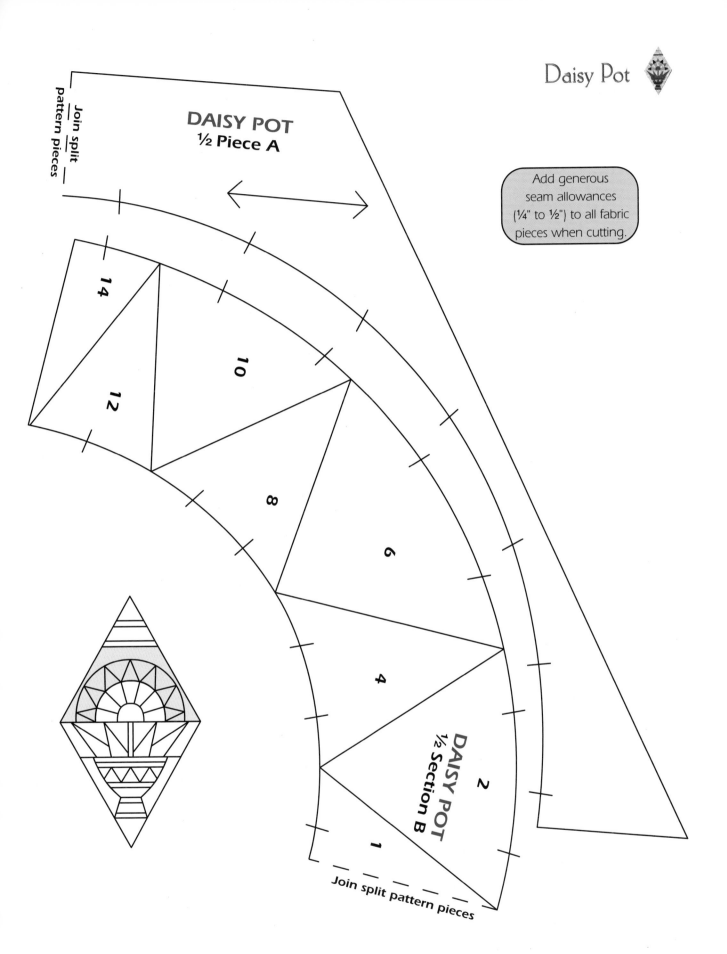

DAISY POT
½ Piece A

Join split
pattern pieces

14

12

10

8

6

4

DAISY POT
½ Section B

2

1

Join split pattern pieces

Daisy Pot

Add generous
seam allowances
(¼" to ½") to all fabric
pieces when cutting.

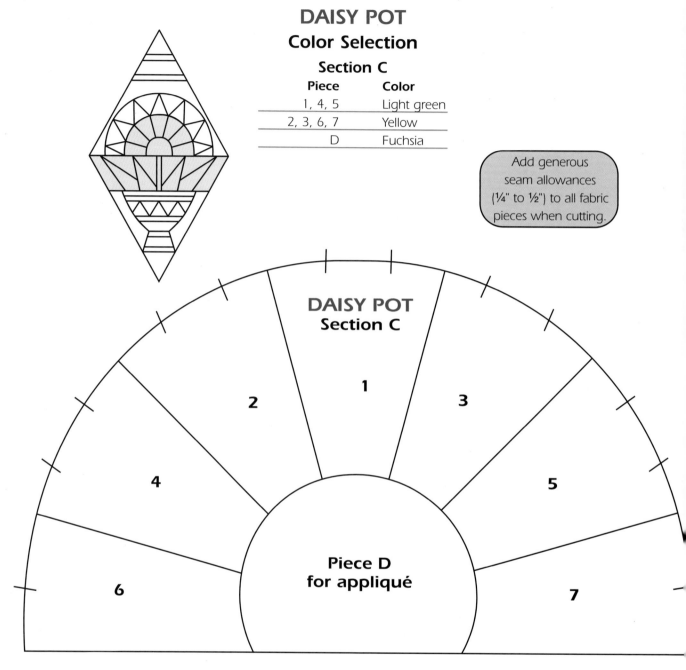

DAISY POT
Color Selection
Section C

Piece	Color
1, 4, 5	Light green
2, 3, 6, 7	Yellow
D	Fuchsia

Add generous seam allowances (¼" to ½") to all fabric pieces when cutting.

DAISY POT
Section C

Piece D
for appliqué

Reverse Appliqué

After piecing C, place Piece D, right side up, onto the fabric side of the foundation piecing, covering D and ensuring a seam allowance all around, but especially at the lower edge. Iron in place. Turn to the paper side and stitch on the line between C and D, through all layers. This method of reverse appliqué works best if you match the bobbin thread to the piece to be appliquéd, in this case the fuchsia used for Piece D.

Turn to the fabric side and trim the appliquéd patch close to the stitching. Now cover the raw edge and the stitching with a satin stitch. This is the quickest, easiest and most accurate way to appliqué patch D, but you can use your own technique if you prefer.

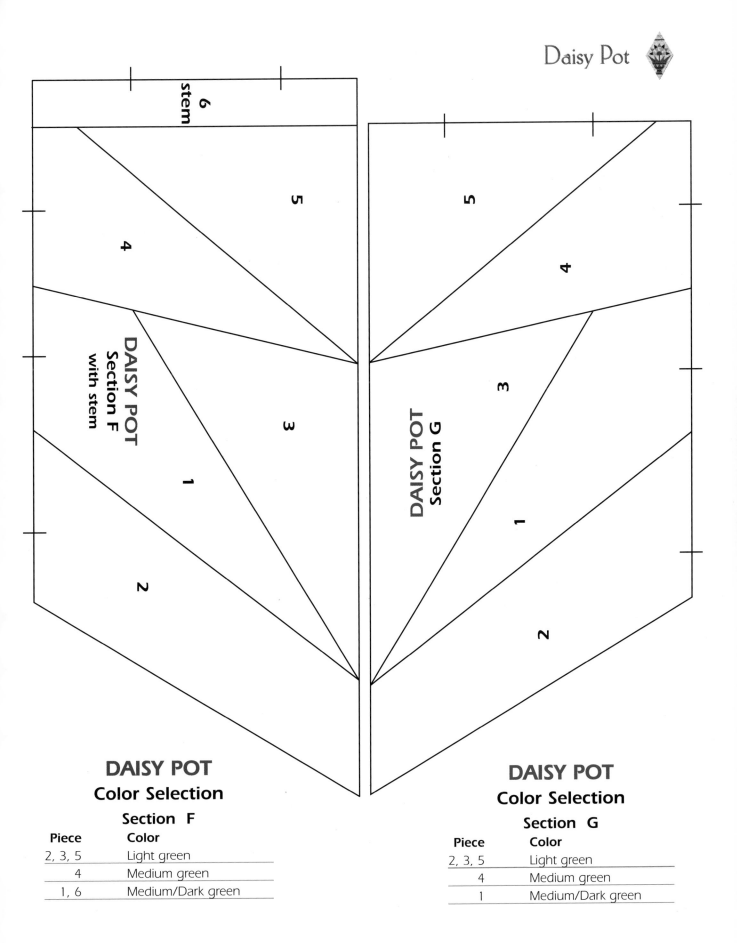

6 stem

5

4

**DAISY POT
Section F
with stem**

3

1

2

5

4

**DAISY POT
Section G**

3

1

2

DAISY POT
Color Selection
Section F

Piece	Color
2, 3, 5	Light green
4	Medium green
1, 6	Medium/Dark green

DAISY POT
Color Selection
Section G

Piece	Color
2, 3, 5	Light green
4	Medium green
1	Medium/Dark green

Daisy Pot

Pot and Leaf Assembly

To make the pot-leaf triangle, foundation piece Sections F and G, and match the marks to join the two sections.

Foundation piece Sections H and I, and curved pieces J and Jr.

Assemble the pot – H, I, J, and Jr – following the method described in the General Instructions.

Sew the leaf part, FG, to the pot part, HIJ.

Join the flowerhead triangle to the pot/leaf triangle, matching marks.

DAISY POT
Color Selection
Section H

Piece	Color
1, 4, 5	Fuchsia
2, 3, 6, 7	Yellow
8, 10	Deep purple
9, 11	Red

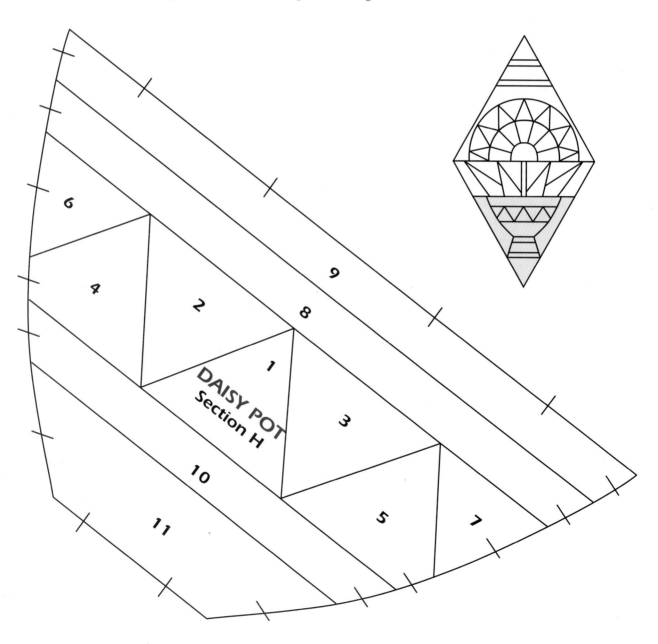

DAISY POT
Color Selection
Section 1

Piece	Color
1	Red
2, 3	Deep purple
4, J, Jr	Light green

Add generous seam allowances (¼" to ½") to all fabric pieces when cutting.

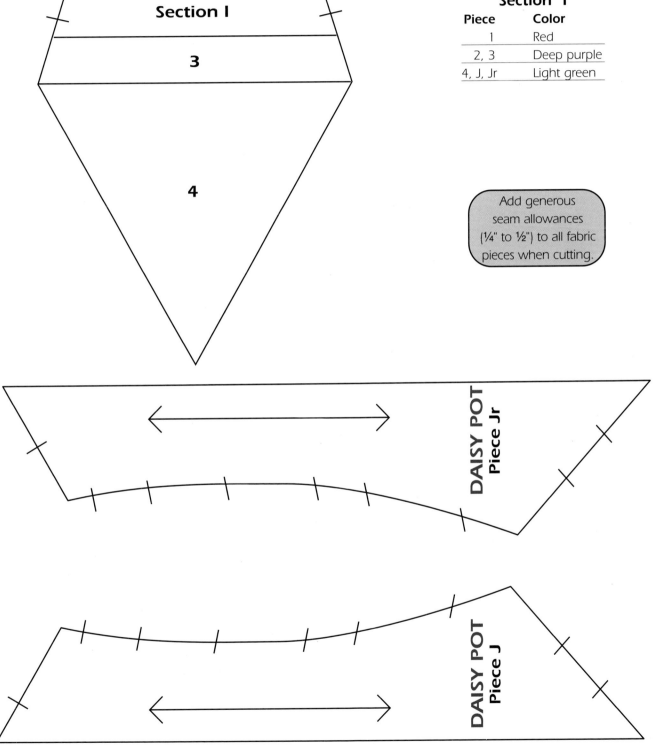

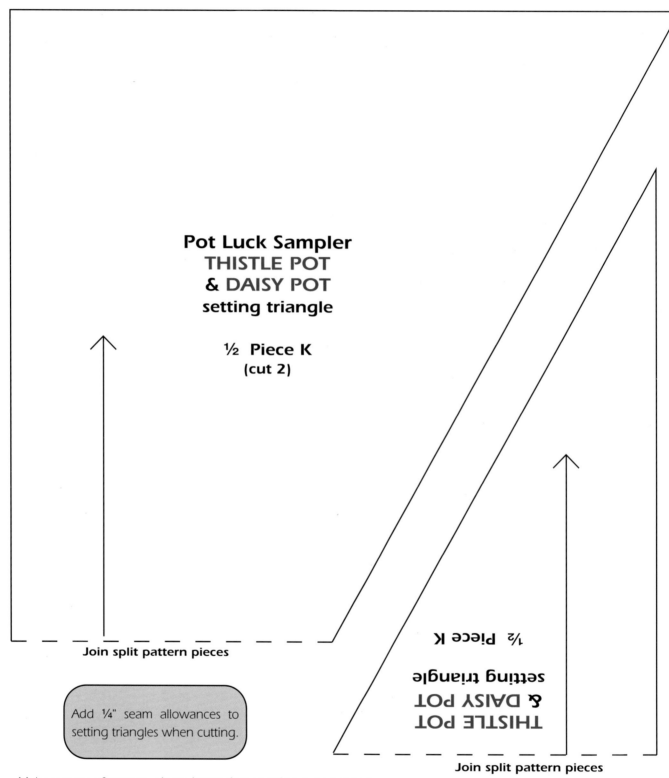

Pot Luck Sampler
THISTLE POT
& DAISY POT
setting triangle

½ Piece K
(cut 2)

Join split pattern pieces

Add ¼" seam allowances to setting triangles when cutting.

½ Piece K

setting triangle
& DAISY POT
THISTLE POT

Join split pattern pieces

Make a copy of pattern pieces by tracing or using a non-distorting photocopier. Join pattern sections on dashed lines as indicated. Make a full-sized master copy of the entire pattern before tracing pattern pieces onto the dull side of freezer paper.

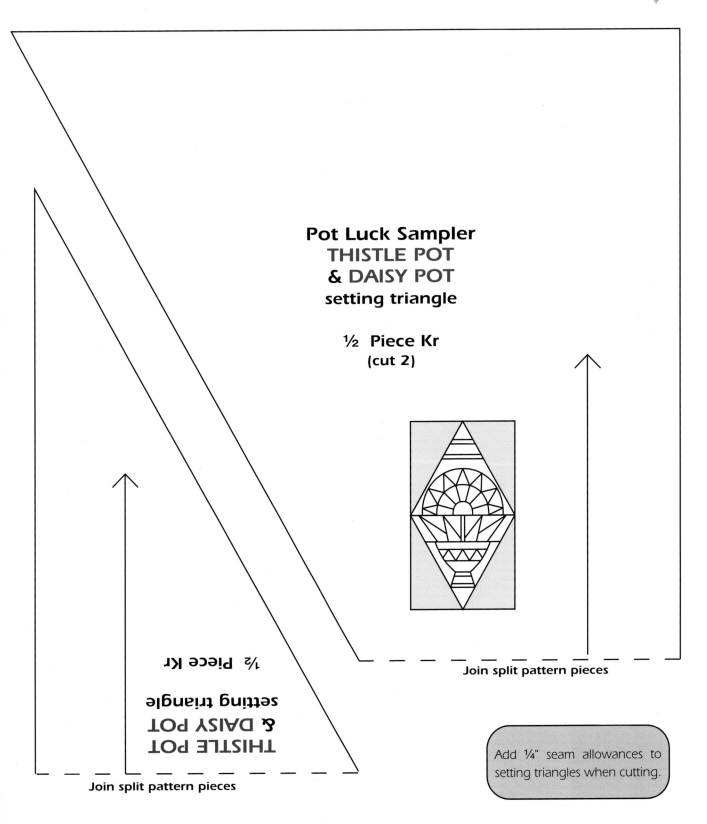

Pot Luck Sampler
THISTLE POT
& DAISY POT
setting triangle

½ Piece Kr
(cut 2)

Join split pattern pieces

½ Piece Kr

setting triangle
THISTLE POT
& DAISY POT

Join split pattern pieces

Add ¼" seam allowances to setting triangles when cutting.

SUNSHINE PATIO
50" x 44"

Six DAISY POTS set with half diamonds make a beautiful tablecloth. The center can be left open to allow the cloth to be slipped over an umbrella pole. Make the DAISY POTS in Christmas fabrics for an unusual tree skirt.

In this quilt, the pot has been cut from striped fabric in one piece, since the fabric design is strong enough to fill the pot template. This is a quick way to make six pots!

CHINESE DAISY
14½" x 25"

The Daisy Pot quilts on the following pages give just an indication of the color schemes possible with this block. Note the varied use of stripes and the different results that contemporary and traditional fabrics give.

CHRISTMAS DAISY
14½" x 25"

Sewn by Jackie Tonks.

Dutch Flower Pot Quilts – Anja Townrow

TRADITIONAL DAISY
14½" x 25"

GOLDEN DAISY
14½" x 25"

Kaleidopot

Block Size 10¾" x 13"

Although not included in POT LUCK SAMPLER, this pattern makes an interesting addition to the Flower Pot collection. Patterns are included to make two stunning quilts using the easy-to-sew Kaleidopot design. The block is made in two parts, a flower Section A or variation Aa, and pot Section B.

AZTEC KALEIDOSCOPE
29" x 29"

Eight blocks (AB) set with corner triangles (C) and borders make this vibrant wallhanging with a South American feel. A spiral appliqué motif in the center adds interest, as do the extensive embroidery and quilting, executed in thick decorative thread.

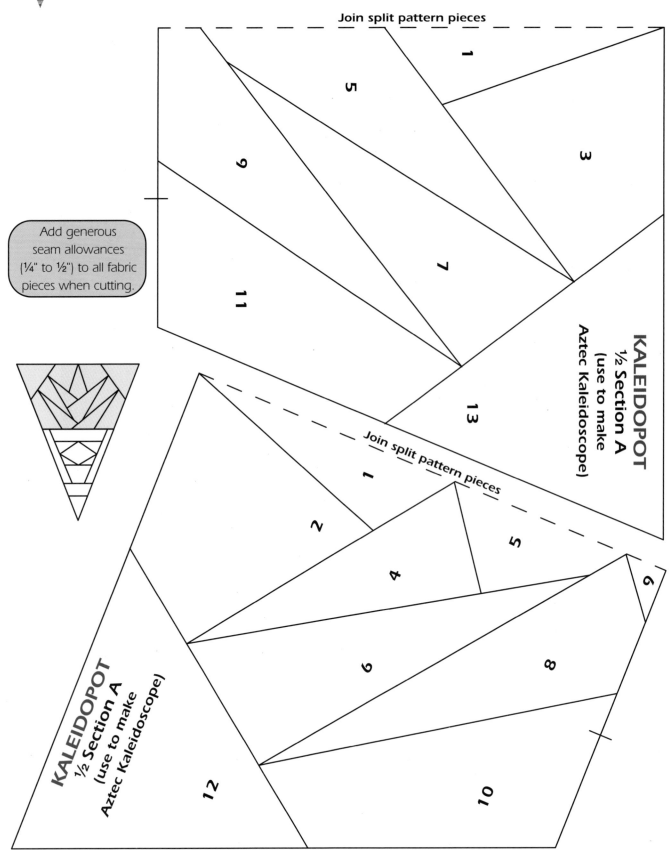

Join split pattern pieces

1

5

3

9

7

11

Add generous
seam allowances
(¼" to ½") to all fabric
pieces when cutting.

13

KALEIDOPOT
½ Section A
(use to make
Aztec Kaleidoscope)

Join split pattern pieces

1

2

4

5

6

9

8

KALEIDOPOT
½ Section A
(use to make
Aztec Kaleidoscope)

12

10

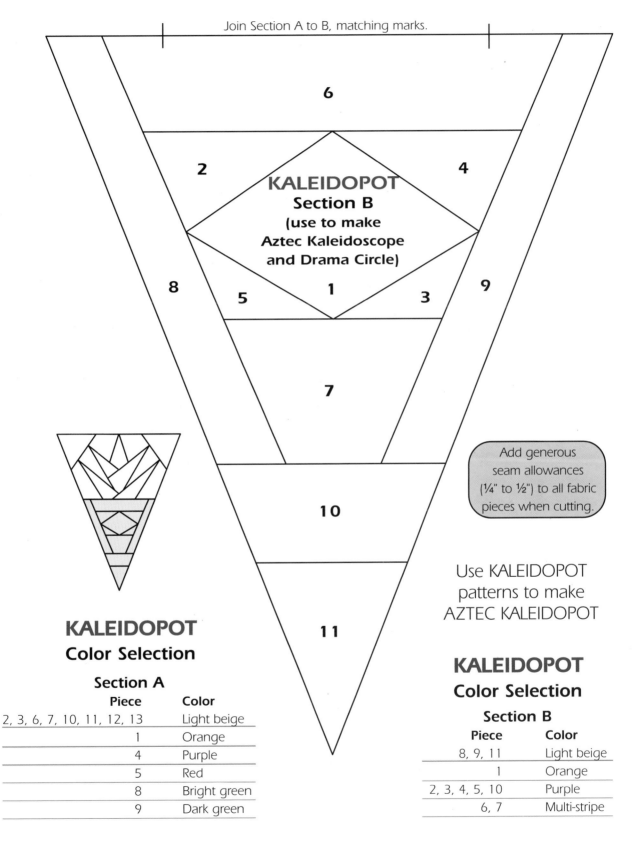

Join Section A to B, matching marks.

6

2

4

KALEIDOPOT
Section B
(use to make
Aztec Kaleidoscope
and Drama Circle)

8

5

1

3

9

7

Add generous
seam allowances
(¼" to ½") to all fabric
pieces when cutting.

10

Use KALEIDOPOT
patterns to make
AZTEC KALEIDOPOT

11

KALEIDOPOT
Color Selection

Section A

Piece	Color
2, 3, 6, 7, 10, 11, 12, 13	Light beige
1	Orange
4	Purple
5	Red
8	Bright green
9	Dark green

KALEIDOPOT
Color Selection

Section B

Piece	Color
8, 9, 11	Light beige
1	Orange
2, 3, 4, 5, 10	Purple
6, 7	Multi-stripe

Kaleidopot

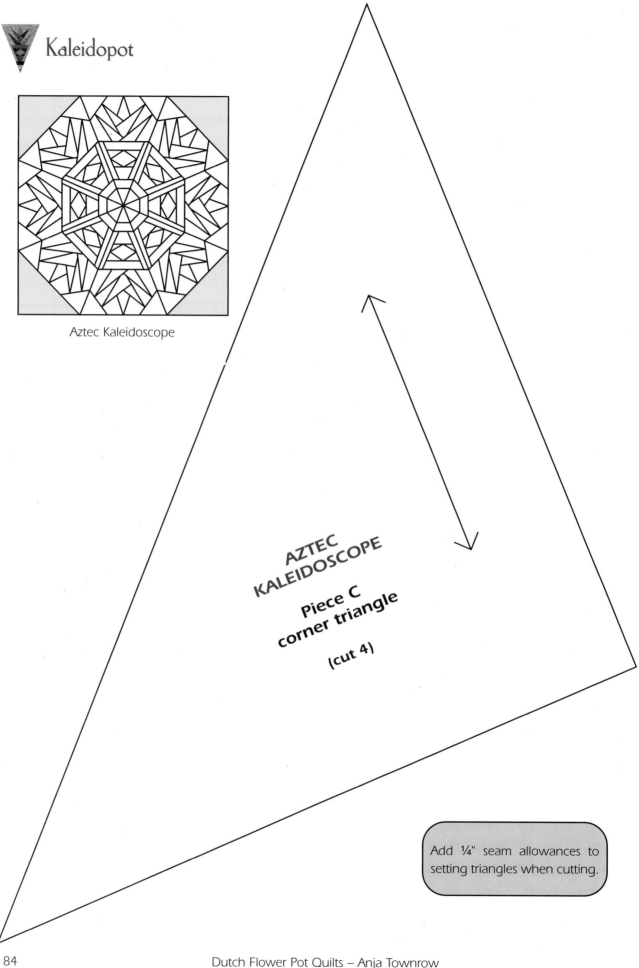

Aztec Kaleidoscope

**AZTEC
KALEIDOSCOPE**

*Piece C
corner triangle*

(cut 4)

Add ¼" seam allowances to setting triangles when cutting.

DRAMA CIRCLE
30" diameter

Eight blocks (AaB) and border D are used to make this quilt. Bright colors on a very dark blue background were used for this version of the block. By foundation piecing the triangle border, you will be able to make this striking design quickly and accurately. Add the border after all the blocks have been joined.

Kaleidopot

Add generous seam allowances (¼" to ½") to all fabric pieces when cutting.

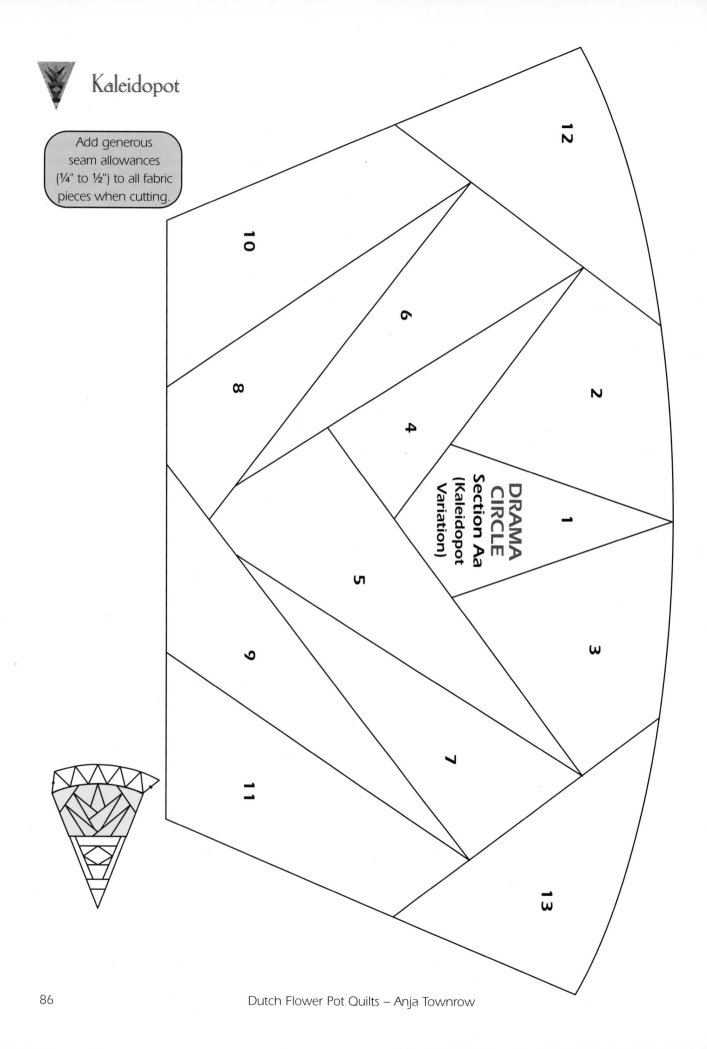

DRAMA CIRCLE
Section Aa
(Kaleidopot Variation)

1 2 3 4 5 6 7 8 9 10 11 12 13

Dutch Flower Pot Quilts – Anja Townrow

Make a copy of pattern pieces by tracing or using a non-distorting photocopier. Join pattern sections on dashed lines as indicated. Make a full-sized master copy of the entire pattern before tracing pattern pieces onto the dull side of freezer paper. Make eight Section Ds for the complete border.

DRAMA CIRCLE
Color Selection
Section Aa

Piece	Color
2, 3, 6, 7, 10, 11, 12, 13	Dark blue
1	Yellow
4	Orange
5	Pink
8	Teal
9	Bright green

DRAMA CIRCLE
Color Selection
Section B
(use pattern on page 83)

Piece	Color
8, 9, 11	Dark blue
1	Teal
2, 3, 4, 5	Orange
6, 7, 10	Multi-stripe

DRAMA CIRCLE
Color Selection
Section D

Piece	Color
2, 3, 6, 7, 10	Dark blue
1	Yellow
4	Pink
5	Orange
8	Bright green
9	Teal

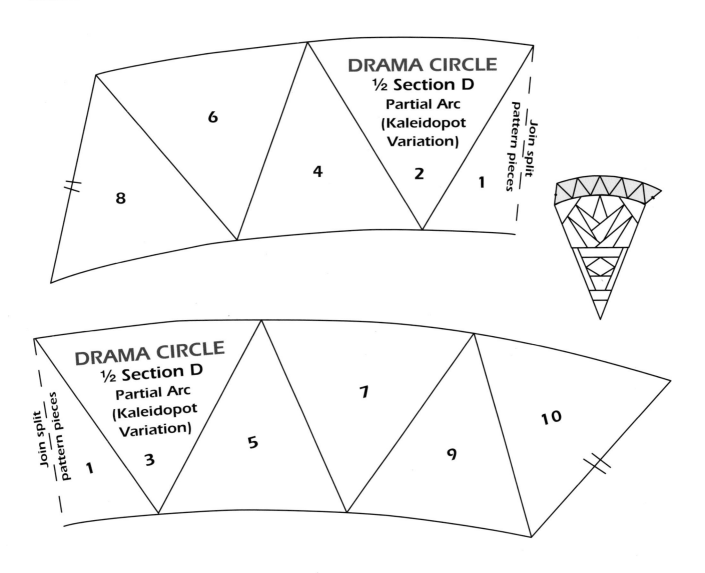

DRAMA CIRCLE
½ Section D
Partial Arc
(Kaleidopot Variation)

Join split pattern pieces

6 · 4 · 2 · 1 · 8

DRAMA CIRCLE
½ Section D
Partial Arc
(Kaleidopot Variation)

Join split pattern pieces

1 · 3 · 5 · 7 · 9 · 10

Pot Noodle

Block Size 9" x 14"

This block was named by my husband, a man who suffers a lot for my "art." After designing and sewing yet another pot block, I took a break and wandered into the living room. There sat Will in his usual pose in front of the TV, hand on the remote control.

"Look," I cried, "here's a new pot but I don't know what to call it." Will did not hesitate or even take his eyes off the screen; his reply was instant and uncannily apt: "POT NOODLE." What would we do without the help and support of our families?

This block consists of two parts: a flower part formed by Section A, and a pot part formed by Section B and pieces C, D, and Dr.

14" x 20". By Jackie Tonks

14" x 20". By Jackie Tonks

14" x 20"

Three one-block quilts are shown here with a variety of borders. Notice how different the block looks when romantic florals are used, as in the quilt above made by Jackie Tonks.

Pot Noodle

Make a copy of pattern pieces by tracing or using a non-distorting photo-copier. Join pattern sections on dashed lines as indicated. Make a full-sized master copy of the entire pattern before tracing pattern pieces onto the dull side of freezer paper.

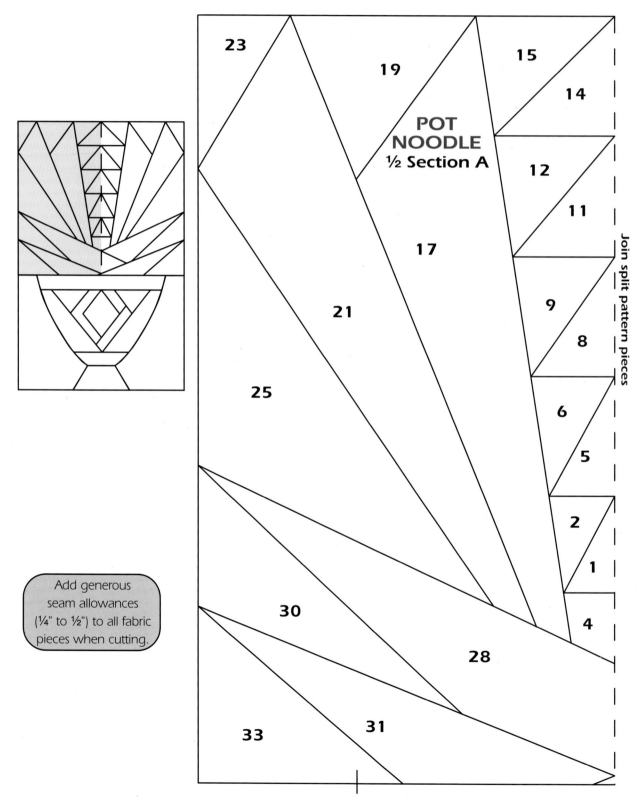

POT NOODLE ½ Section A

Join split pattern pieces

Add generous seam allowances (¼" to ½") to all fabric pieces when cutting.

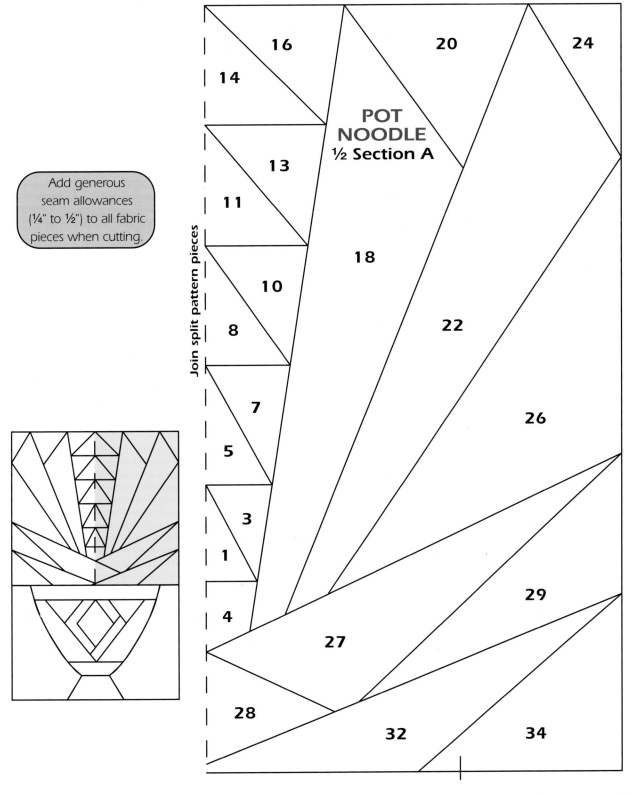

Add generous seam allowances (¼" to ½") to all fabric pieces when cutting.

Join split pattern pieces

POT NOODLE
½ Section A

16
14
20
24
13
11
18
10
22
8
26
7
5
3
1
4
27
29
28
32
34

Pot Noodle

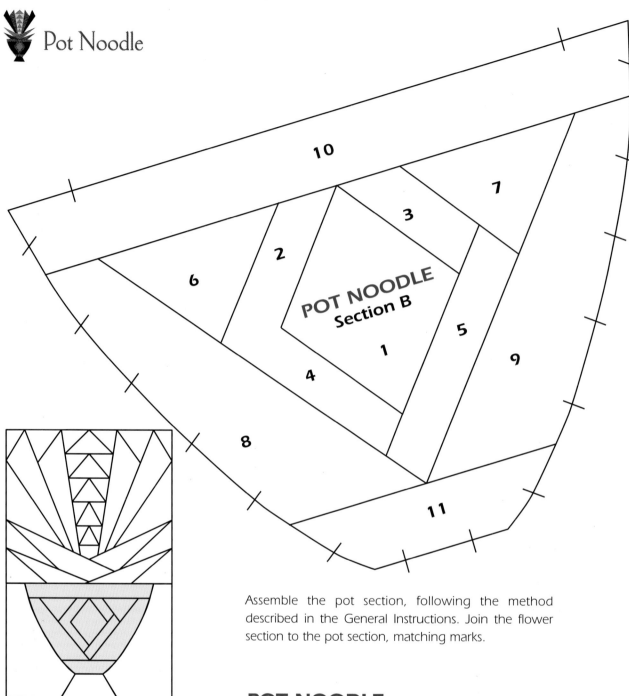

Assemble the pot section, following the method described in the General Instructions. Join the flower section to the pot section, matching marks.

POT NOODLE
Color Selection

Section A	
Piece	**Color**
2, 3, 4, 6, 7, 9, 10, 12, 13, 15, 16, 19, 20, 23, 24, 25, 26, 29, 30, 33, 34	Yellow
1, 5, 8, 11, 14	Orange
17, 18	Black/white stripe
21, 22	Black
27, 28	Bright green
31, 32	Dark green

Section B	
Piece	**Color**
1	Orange
2, 3, 4, 5, 10, 11	Black/white stripe
6, 7, 8, 9, C	Black
D, Dr	Yellow

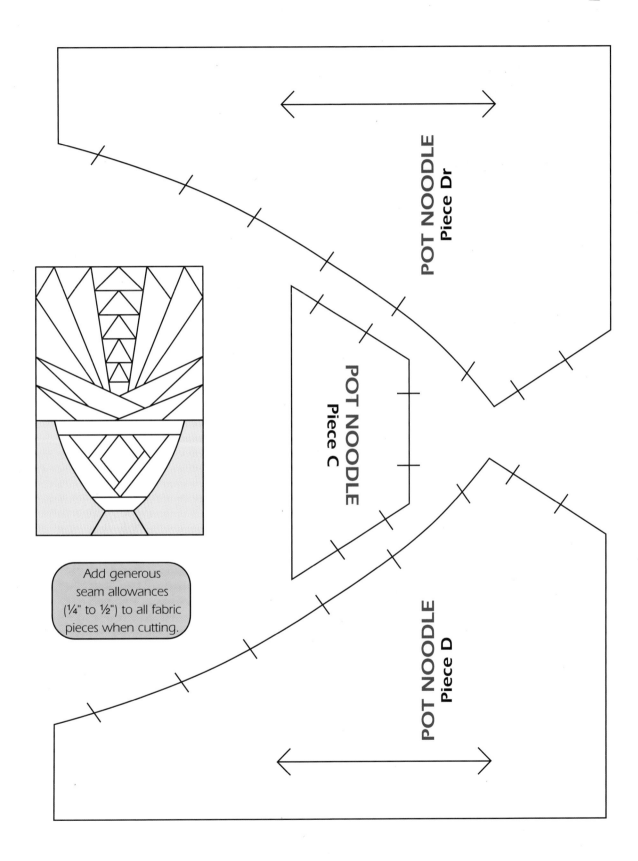

POT NOODLE
Piece Dr

POT NOODLE
Piece C

POT NOODLE
Piece D

Add generous seam allowances (¼" to ½") to all fabric pieces when cutting.

Pot Noodle Variations

TROPICAL HOTPOTS 32" x 17"

POT NOODLE is included in this small wallhanging made with batik fabrics. When using striking fabrics like these, you need only select a few for maximum impact.

FRESCO POTS 36" x 20"

The colors in this quilt are reminiscent of the fresco paintings seen on walls in Mediterranean countries. Compare this quilt with TROPICAL HOTPOTS to see the enormous difference the choice of fabric can have on a design.

About the Author

Anja Townrow was born in The Hague, Holland, and grew up in a village in the Dutch Polderland. After studying English language and literature at the University of Leiden, she moved to England in 1974. Since the late 1980s when quilting magazines and books from the United States became more widely available in the United Kingdom, she has been greatly inspired by American quilters.

Anja is a self-taught quiltmaker who has won many prizes for her work. She travels extensively, teaching in Britain and Europe. Known for her use of vibrant colors, Anja's ever-expanding range of patterns is produced under the name of Dutch Quilts, and her designs can also be found as regular contributions in various patchwork publications.

Anja has three daughters, whose ages range from 8 to 22, so perhaps it's not surprising that after fitting the school run, visits to the gym, and quilting into her day, she frequently forgets to water her plants!

For more information about Dutch Quilt patterns and quilts, visit Anja's website at www.anjatownrow.com.

OTHER AQS BOOKS

AQS books are known worldwide for timely topics, clear writing, beautiful color photos, and accurate illustrations and patterns. This is only a small selection of the books available from your local bookseller, quilt shop or public library.

#5754   US $19.95

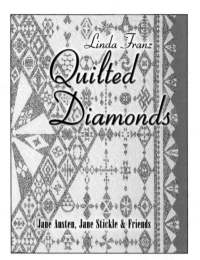

#5847   US $24.95

#5756   US $19.95

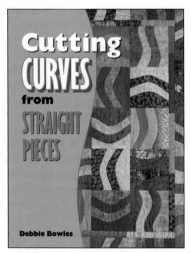

#5755   US $21.95

#5852   US $19.95

#4594   US $18.95

#5761   US $22.95

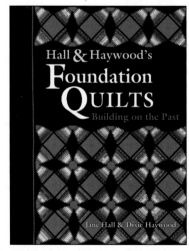

#5707   US $26.95

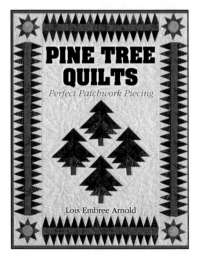

#5708   US $22.95

Look for these books nationally or call **1-800-626-5420**